A Serial Poem

D1520014

Also by Daryl Hine

Poetry:
Recollected Poems: 1951-2004 (2007)
Postscripts (1991)
In & Out (1989)
Arrondisements (1988)
Academic Festival Overtures (1985)
Selected Poems (1980)
Daylight Saving (1978)
Bluebeard's Wife (1976)
Resident Alien (1975)
Minutes (1968)
The Wooden Horse (1965)
Heroics (1960)
The Devil's Picture Book (1962)
The Carnal and the Crane (1957)
Five Poems (1954)

Translation:
Works of Hesiod and the Homeric Hymns (2005)
Puerilities: Erotic Epigrams of the Greek Anthology (2001)
Ovid's Heroines: A Verse Translation of the Heroides (1991)
Theocritus: Idylls and Epigrams (1982)

Prose:
Polish Subtitles (1962)
The Prince of Darkness & Co. (1961)

A Serial Poem

Daryl Hine

Fitzhenry & Whiteside

&: A Serial Poem
Copyright © 2010 Daryl Hine

Fitzhenry and Whiteside Limited
195 Allstate Parkway, Markham, Ontario L3R 4T8

In the United States:
311 Washington Street, Brighton, Massachusetts 02135

www.fitzhenry.ca godwit@fitzhenry.ca

Fitzhenry & Whiteside acknowledges with thanks the Canada Council for the Arts, and the Ontario Arts Council for their support of our publishing program. We acknowledge the financial support of the Government of Canada through the Book Publishing Industry Development Program (BPIDP) for our publishing activities.

Library and Archives Canada Cataloguing in Publication
Hine, Daryl, 1936-
& : a serial poem / Daryl Hine.
ISBN 978-1-55455-164-4
I. Title. II. Title: Ampersand.
PS8515.I5A75 2010   C811'.54   C2010-900222-9

United States Cataloguing-in-Publication Data
Hine, Daryl.
& : a serial poem / Daryl Hine.
[112] p. : cm.
Summary: A series of three-hundred, ten-line lyric poems, linked by and flowing through the ampersand.
ISBN: 978-1-55455-164-4 (pbk.)
1. Canadian poetry – 21st century.   2. Lyric poetry, Canadian – 21st century.
I. Title.
811.6 dc22   PS3608.I6An   2010

Cover and interior design by Intuitive Design International Ltd.
Printed and bound in Canada

1 3 5 7 9 10 8 6 4 2

For Will

&

In Memory of Sam

CONTENTS

&: A Serial Poem ... [9]

Notes ... [110]

Acknowledgements ... [111]

Ampersand = "and per se and"
— Oxford English Dictionary

1

What if one waited & it never came,
Save for an inflammation in the East,
A faint illumination that increased
Till the expected day flared into flame,
& what was yesterday today became
The unaltered altar of an immoveable feast,
As if through a narrow opening one saw
Everything changed & everything the same,
Not yet remembered because not yet deceased.
Non omnia omina in anima.

2

An iridescent, precious filament
Underlines the migratory fly-way
Where no constructs obstruct the high-flown highway,
Till heaven knows where all that splendour went
Minutes later! Under my wonderment
At unwilling pleasure, condemned to getting my way,
I treasure dawn's opal, tourmaline & topaz,
Before sun-up, & wonder what that wonder meant,
Dawn's nascent, incandescent by-way.
Is it harder to get what one wants, or to want what one has?

3

Daybreak to dawn like triumph to victory
After an inauspicious interval
Succeeds, to signify our eventual
Retreat from an unsatisfactory
Night campaign whose valedictory
Enlightenment is becoming visible
As the doors of darkness slowly shut
Upon a conundrum, which introductory
Paradox becomes a parable:
When a symbol is not a symbol? If nothing but.

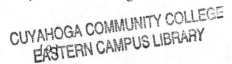

4

Across Discovery Bay the dawn came stealing,
Donning again the helmet of the will
With willful fulfillments too facile to fulfill,
Steadily, its stealthy beams revealing
Up on the screen of the shadow-embattled ceiling,
A skiamachia that never will be still.
Baffling, black & white & bountiful
Marvels unanticipated began to spill
From copious cornucopias of feeling:
How can one fill what evermore is full?

5

Across Recovery Bay the sun came stealing,
Surreptitiously creeping up out of the deep,
Breaking & entering into my brittle sleep,
To censor the phantasmal film unreeling
Beneath the eyelids' hovering, cloudy ceiling,
Nocturnal images too ephemeral to keep,
& as an explorer inadvertently discovered
This placid inlet, awakening a feeling
Of daring not to look before you leap
Ashore on a landfall like a lover lightly covered.

6

Waking too often, too often waking early
As sunrise cast its shadow on the sky,
Through swirling curtains of furious flurries I
Reconstitute imperfectly & obscurely
Dreams as deliquescent as the pearly
Flakes wept away as soon as they went awry,
Disconcerted to awake again
To the certainty that that's that, that surely
Bygones will, like this blizzard, have gone by,
& eventually every loss will prove a gain.

7

Insignificantly, in florid indecision,
Dazed, the daystar rises by degrees
Athwart the horizon, as a diffident breeze
Disturbs the curtains to unveil a vision
As astonishing as a decision:
Indeterminate beyond the opening, a frieze
Of freezing trees not frozen. Will this frigid season
Of rehabilitation & revision
Open a frosted window through which one sees
The dark night of the soul become the dawn of reason?

8

Will the risen sun remember its descent,
While the lucidity demanded by the day
Lingers as long as latent light's decay,
Till the orient blends into the occident
To dissolve into its dissolute element,
As a floating boat floats everyone away:
Trahit sua quemque voluptas?
Or, when pleasure proves impermanent,
Will omnipotent will lead one & all astray:
Trahit sua quemque voluntas?

9

Experimental as fission through thin ice
In a thermonuclear desert overcast
By unclear winter, suspended above a vast
Surprise by an elementary device,
Gripped in retrospect as in an icy vice
By images passionately unsurpassed,
Remembrance angles for a forgotten place
Imprisoned in that glacial paradise,
Till like an unexpected catch, the past
Suddenly ups & smacks you in the face.

10

When nowadays every night suggests surrender
&, near the frontiers of consciousness, defeat,
Reality's realm & phantasmagoria meet
In a no-man's land devoid of age or gender
Where an irresponsible pretender
& impossible probabilities compete
For a dark continent half undiscovered,
Luxurious, calm, voluptuous & tender,
Without which no expedition would be complete,
Above which the mourning doves of lost love hovered.

11

That was the year's & this unreason's midnight,
Unforgettable, neither the last nor first
Yet the longest, the dirtiest & the worst
Eclipse, a hidden, hideously humid night
Waiting for false dawn, a fake sunburst amid night
Shadows & psychodramas over-rehearsed.
In the soul's solstice nothing seems what it seems,
Nor can you remember what you did night
After night, when revelations are reversed
By morning. There are no witnesses in dreams.

12

Bright before my eyes, a surprise white-out
Amid winter light outside, in the glary glow
& pallid penumbra of the purblind snow
Draws a blank after a white night out
On the inner passage. Why not light out
For the territory where no frozen rivers flow,
A country of precognitive conditions,
Absolutely nowhere, out of sight, out
This window, where suicidal blizzards blow
& space & time exist as superstitions?

13

Never weary of the cycle of the seasons,
How often tired of the order of the day
Minutely as it varies day-by-day,
As melancholy survivors we all see suns
Rise & set for inexplicable reasons.
Minutes fidget; few would one invite to stay.
Ephemeral, quotidian, diurnal
Hours not ours, whose trivial trite treasons
Leave the years with little to betray,
Diversify earth's eternally turning journal.

14

A spontaneous spectacular effusion
Erupts abruptly through earth's cratered crust;
Glowing lava flows, sluggardly as lust
Unslaked, down slabby slopes amid confusion
Of fire & fear & *furioso* fusion,
As mountainsides & trees & rocks combust
With every element save H_2O,
Including the air. Renewal & conclusion,
Smothered with dust & ashes & disgust,
A new volcano percolates below.

15

Words cannot describe that may evoke
Natural landscapes like this placid valley
Through which glassy streamlets glance & dally
Dully, & shadowy cataracts gleam like smoke
Down majestic mountains clad in a cloudy cloak.
Yet every evocation seems virtually
Commonplace as the depictions that we keep
To ourselves in a language no one spoke,
A dreamy idiolect in which we shilly-shally,
Waking up before we go to sleep.

16

Nothing if not an indispensable envelope
For memorabilia, amused
By nothing, a medium to be used,
Spent or wasted like a bar of soap
That will outlast us, or an endless rope,
A gratuity that cannot be refused
Unlike such synchronicities as rhyme,
Time passes anyway, sometimes a slope
We scramble down, disheveled & confused,
Sometimes a winding stair up which we climb.

17

As often a day as one drifts off to sleep
So many times a night might one awake.
Unconsciousness is nothing one can fake:
Who knows the moment when he falls asleep
At last? We cannot look before we leap,
Yet recognize the instant when we wake
As often literally breath-taking.
While the descent was slow so the ascent is steep,
Immediately revealed as a mistake.
Soon there will be no more sleep & no more waking,

18

Startled, we will not stir, nor, shaken, wake
From our obligatory oblivion.
Darkness may shrink & blush before the dawn
Unseen, but day will never break
Upon our senses, nor sun rise for our sake
Once all our susceptibilities are gone
Amiss, & what appeared mere oversight
Reveals itself time & again as a mistake—
Immaterial, seeing that no light has ever shone
On this eternal dormitory night.

19

The clock the day unwinds winds up the dreamwork
of the night
Watch. In an hiatus between never & not yet
Denial dies: neither to remember nor forget
Altogether, almost or not quite,
That sorrow was after all just sorrow, not delight.
Though the greatest griefs are said eventually to get
Better, they might well become inevitably worse.
Innumerable lacunae blackly punctuate tonight,
As numerals, the letters of the devil's alphabet,
Accumulate till they begin to count down in reverse.

20

To eavesdrop on your irreversibly aging
Inner strictures, listen to a sundial tick
On & off, too often all too quick,
Sometimes simply stuck. Obsessively try paging
Through a secular book of hours, & disengaging
Minutes from the days to which they stick
As entries in a preliminary, secret index
That indicates another way of gauging
Time's invincible arithmetic
Under the sub-heading, *Tempus Vindex*.

21

High in the heavens' motion circular
(Or approximately elliptical), concentric
Orbits delineate a geocentric
Jigsaw puzzle whose missing pieces are
Insignificant, each narcissistic star
Of whatever magnitude, an egocentric
Fragment of conspicuous disorder,
The magnificent, inexplicable, bizarre,
Spectacle, necessarily eccentric,
Of first things first, not always in that order.

22

Sifting down through twisted and entangled
Vegetative interrelationships,
A slippery illumination slips
Day-long, insinuating, mangled
Among paw-paws, orchids & bananas dangled
Between passion-flowers' pouting lips.
Far above the rankness of this old-fangled jungle-gym
A gazillion uninteresting star-spangled
Voids fill the invisible sky with alien spaceships,
While in the dismal dimness quetzals mate & crocodiles
      swim.

23

What if there were no life beyond the stars,
No further folderol but cosmic dust
Among the planets' destined wanderlust,
No gas stations & no go-go bars
Where Venus, Saturn, Mercury & Mars
May hang out, who move because they must
To demonstrate their negligible worth
As imaginary avatars?
The heavens are dumb, but nonetheless we trust
That there is intelligent life on earth.

24

An overseer too faint-hearted to illumine
Much, away or scarcely there most days,
Daily veiled by the blaze of noon as by a haze
Of unshed tears & vaporized bitumen,
Gazing down unfazed but not unphased, inhuman,
Reflecting on humans' unreflecting ways,
The shy, crescent-shaped & not unsung young moon,
Obnoxious to sunlight, literally *lumen*
De lumine, "light from light", taints with her faint rays
A sublunary landscape, doomed to fade into daylight soon.

25

That ghastly ghost, a pock-marked luminary,
Squinting down with frigid upper class
Disdain on our mundane, morose morass,
& its dead-beat denizens, although not very
Bright, reflects a pallid secondary
Light upon this sublunary addable mass;
Serene above the earth as a balloon,
A body more decorative than necessary,
With waterless seas & plains of pitted glass,
Shines the otherworldly beauty of the moon.

26

This UFO that landed on my desk
Has no mind inside its uncritical apparatus,
Nor body neither. & no divine afflatus,
Merely a mechanical burlesque
Of reason, replacing the archaic, arabesque
Penmanship that used to exasperate us,
A manuscript rewritten never to be reread,
As impervious as picturesque,
Deserving almost the legendary status
Of letters semi-legible, cool & technically undead.

27

Conning my letters from Prince Valiant
In the comic pages, preliterate perforce
Before four, I drew from some primordial source
Each liquid vowel & arid consonant
To spell out the course of an erotic, significant
Story, self-educated by the force
Of narrative that fascinates me yet.
With all the studious patience of an ant,
Absorbed in that inexhaustible resource,
I attempted to reinvent the alphabet.

28

Semiotic as an alphabet in short
Hand or long, what code can explicate
An orthography that makes the crooked straight,
Script as predictable as a weather report,
Mute as music, serious as sport,
& candid as a political candidate?
The secret lies in learning to address
Whatever recourses fiction may resort
To &, however inaccurately, translate,
Writing that fits its subject like a dress.

29

Everyone authorizes his own bible
As revised & plagiarized by everyman,
A book of books or a library that began
With *Genesis*, not creation, as a tribal
Tract, a prosaic monomaniac libel
In many mistranslations, absent an
Original or any definitive text.
This inspired tissue of lies ascribed to scribal
Error has no plot but a master plan
As an authoritative guide for the perplexed.

30

No standard handbooks of revelations cite
Such undocumented & arbitrary
Miracles as abound in any dictionary,
Whose odd, forgotten etymologies might
Rewrite the irregular rules of wrong & right,
As fluid & altogether unnecessary
As the sources of language's hydra-headed fountain,
While night after night we wordlessly recite
Redefinitions founded in faith's reliquary
Which, God willing, might remove a mountain.

31

Dictionaries fail, definitions founder.
From mysterious midden & inconspicuous mound
Hints half-hidden like flints stick up out of the ground
Of common speech, folk etymologies no sounder
Than they sound, along with platitudes profounder
Than the hackneyed misinterpretations that surround
& corrupt the plundered word horde's stereotypical stores.
Through argosies of pseudo-synonyms we flounder
After the profound significance to be found
In clichés that masquerade as metaphors.

32

A simile, unlike your metaphor,
However far-fetched, is generally true,
Though both do all comparisons can do,
Opening a figurative back door
Onto vistas often visited before,
Now a view comparatively new
Of some figurative beauty spot
Too mundane & unimportant to ignore.
Though there are a few similitudes like you,
An acceptable facsimile there is not.

33

Omnia vincit amor, a euphemism,
As so many explanations are,
For the motor in the back seat of the car,
An eternal combustion engine silly as a syllogism,
Reined in by the intelligence of my shining avatar,
Till, at the entropic edge of cataclysm,
Everything ends as clutch comes to shove.
Urn within urn! As a neologism,
Another word for an exploding star,
Give me if you will a synonym for love.

34

In our language *you* is not declined,
Though *I* & *we* & *he* are all inflected
Case by case, objectively subjected
To the sentimental grammar of the mind,
Defining relations otherwise ill-defined
Or effecting connections better disconnected.
Whether as subject or object the only true
Exemplary paradigm of your own kind,
You are the singular person I selected,
Who could not love you if you were not you.

35

You may be used not exclusively as the second
Person singular, but as the third
Or first, depending on the identity referred
To. Your personal pronouns generically reckoned
As impersonal persons in a nanosecond
Interpenetrate, their personalities blurred.
All the same, you impersonate no other
One except the unique self that beckoned
Me to you without a superfluous word
In the dialect we use for one another.

36

Talking to yourself in the second person,
A universal solitary vice,
Giving oneself good marks & bad advice,
Often inadvertently in blank verse in
Sprung rhythm, like all habits tends to worsen
With age & the need to tell yourself everything twice.
The mindless maledictions that you mumble
Under your breath envisage the unperson
You once were in some extinct paradise
When & wherever. Whatever the matter, you needn't grumble.

37

Persons apart, voices, moods & tenses
Embellish your verb, where no other tense
But here & now imperfectly implements
Simple presents with historical pretenses
Which exemplify the indifference of the senses
To experience, evidence & common sense.
What infinitive can incorporate the essence,
Independent of temporal defenses,
Of the exemplary paradox that represents
You in your impenitent evanescence?

38

Reexamined, the inestimable present
The present intended presently to present
As if some unpresentable presence had sent
It, suggests an expensive yet unpleasant
Putrescent scent together with omnipresent
Emptiness, no content to be content
With; when opened there is nothing in it
Except repentance, which prevents all pleasant
Second guesses, wherever the sentiment
Went whose absence is measured by the minute.

39

Easy-going English knows no moods,
Though *hopefully* figures as that optative
Hopeless native speakers cannot live
Naïve lives without. What interludes
Of hope subjunctive make-believe intrudes
Upon an everyday alternative
Those exiled from felicity endure!
A sort of northerly morning twilight broods
Over the matter-of-fact indicative
Of living as distinct from literature.

40

Too many rhymes! So many coincidences,
Multiple circumstances which coincide,
As if one would ever let identity decide
What property is delineated by our defenses,
The poverty that is defined by our pretences,
As humility is circumscribed by pride.
Sunk in some treacherous reflecting pool,
Seduced by the evidence of his six senses;
Narcissus committed artistic suicide
As a self-deluded rhyming fool.

41

Down a strophic staircase ever turning
Itself into a stanzaic waiting room
Whose polygonal walls like polyphonic rhymes entomb
Dumb yearnings in a catafalque of learning,
Uncertain, inadvertently discerning,
Staggered sentences stumble to resume
A scheme to unwind inevitable-seeming
Verses & reverses eternally returning
For further refurbishment of the verbal tomb
Where your unawakened, perfect life lies dreaming.

42

In this multifaceted diagram every line
Ending echolaically chimes,
Erecting an exoskeleton of rhymes
Of which a thread of meaning forms the spine,
Its traditional, neoclassical design,
Hermetic yet mercurial, trite sometimes,
Predicted by linguistic happenstance.
Such fabricated memories redefine
Arbitrarily other measures, other times,
Leaving not quite everything to chance.

43

Accidental, perchance coincidental,
Similar syllables tinkle, clink & clang,
Echoes corresponding until they boomerang,
Alike despite surprising fundamental
Unlikenesses. With just such sentimental
Affinities the primitive forest rang
Until the prehistoric record stuck.
Repetition possessed such elemental
Charm we did not reflect before we sang
The praises of chance apotheosized as luck.

44

A handy rhyme scheme might provide a map
To guide a body down an indented road
Flash floods of feeling suddenly erode,
Though prosy tourists condemn it as a trap
Laid by many a metrical mishap
& baited by semantic overload,
A way to make the lay of the land explicit
As yesterday asleep in tomorrow's lap.
That prescient & reminiscent code
You may scrape along without, but you will miss it.

45

Mind your step! No body needs no map
To find its footing on this perdition road.
Watching out for supersensory overload,
A happy accident, a fortunate mishap.
One false turn will bring the sloppy slap
Up against a happenstance no signpost showed
A way round: wit's end. You cannot miss it.
Yes, yesterday dozing in tomorrow's lap
Left insufficient instructions in a code
One misstep today may make explicit.

46

Mistiming your psychometrical exercises,
Why bypass those silent, unanalyzed
Asides it would be wise not to be surprised
By, a minefield alive with implied surprises?
While the line like a trampoline subsides & rises,
Its tension is never too tightly synchronized
Over time to time & again revise,
Stylized in as many & manifold disguises
As the divine, as sublimely authorized,
Whose delights we might lack the insight to recognize.

47

If every answer presupposed a question
What goal can preexist without a quest
In which the body's uncomfortable guest,
Subject to ascetic autosuggestion,
Rejects the very sensible suggestion
The suggestible senses are tempted to suggest.
Except for that interesting second guess
Independent of all inquisitive ingestion,
Irrepressible because already guessed,
An unmentionable answer registers a yes.

48

In subtle conundrums such as trouble, some
Insoluble, somewhat inadequate appears
The clue one has been grubbing for for years
Of tribulation, & so troublesome,
Coming up with nothing but a minimum
Number of dumb conjectures numb with tears,
Like all clumsy adumbrations somehow absurd
As an unbecoming triumph, some tiresome sum
Summoned up just as the puzzle disappears
To discover a certain person, the perfect word.

49

Volatile & vulnerable as a bird
That alighted interrogatively shaking
Shoddy plumage as a tawdry dawn was breaking,
An epiphany less apparent than inferred,
Not quite imaginary nor unheard,
Benediction descended as I lay half waking,
In sight at last, forever out of touch,
Instantly welcome & welcomed without a word,
Whose unique nature there was no mistaking,
Unparalleled of its kind, a phoenix, a nonesuch.

50

Ignorant in the burgeoning back yard
With its exuberant foliage & scatty birdsong,
This atonal, garrulous, absurd song,
Untranslatable as that of some vatic bard,
The vernacular of paradise, is hard
To understand—inarticulate, without-words-song,
Spontaneous & innocent of lies,
Which naturally we tend to disregard,
Approximates the eternally unheard song
That is the rhapsody of paradise.

51

The description of some dumb things as poetic,
As in moonlight & "the poetry of motion",
Reflects a vague, ineffable emotion
Indefinite but definitely aesthetic,
Deriving distantly from the pathetic
Fallacy, a preposterous promotion
Of the commonplace to the sublime, inverse
To its demotion to an everyday, bathetic
Notion. Devoid of any emotional lotion,
The only motion of poetry inheres in verse.

52

What prospect rumpled as a dressing-gown.
Some cluttered landfill too crumpled to reduce
To anything like landscape, has any earthly use
As perspective unless upside-down?
For swirls before pine, a muted palette of brown
& grey produces the hues to reproduce
This view of the trees, the moving stream, the season.
One must learn how to swim if only in order to drown
In art, which seemed less a reason than an excuse,
But turns out to be not an excuse but a reason.

53

This frivolous river arisen from some unknown source,
To fall all but forgotten into oblivious ocean,
Uncommonly calm, sometimes becomes a commotion,
Frothy as gossip; often obvious, its course
Runs rapid & shallow, no placid reservoir, a resource
For rumour, that autointoxicating potion
Whose effects are chimerical. Rising out of nowhere,
Exhausted in a season, fame's eddies reinforce
The echo effects of remorseless self-promotion,
Before it ebbs away obscurely, we do not know where.

54

No fastness but a fly-by-night pavilion
Through whose flimsy partitions & filigree windows flit,
Like makeshift similes that ill-befit
Verdant distances with various vermilion
Instinct, insipid images by the zillion,
Is the situation of unconscious omniscience: It.
Into your naive & superstitious
Sleep slither such insidious, reptilian
Insinuations as dreams can counterfeit,
Veridicalities & contradictory wishes.

55

That time will come when a desiccate desert needs
Rain distilled like teardrops from a cloud,
& for the whining wind to weep aloud
In grief as the disbelieving season breeds
Brief relief that springs incontinent as weeds,
As precious & precocious & as proud.
In the rank & blooming wilderness
Each delicate, buried seed succeeds
In burgeoning where growth seemed disallowed,
Under a sodden breeze that whispers, "Nonetheless...".

56

Tomorrow older than today may get
Up disinclined to look back over his shoulder
On hopes leftover & promises grown colder,
Yet not ready to be obliterated yet
Or tucked away in some folder under *Forget*.
How much that touched this infatuate beholder
Plus all the other bric-a-brac love broke
Must rust forgotten in an oubliette
As remembered embers mumble & smoulder,
Smoke without fire where once there was fire without smoke.

57

Unapologetic as rock, as water pure,
Stolid as stone, perspicuous as ice,
& like a glacier impervious to advice,
While immature as early spring you were
Unsure of insuring yourself a sinecure
Yet assured of the virtues of averted vice
As no worse than an imperfect humankindness,
A kind of reincarnation or caricature
Of your kind, which the sundial, a device
For dialing the sun, revises in silent blindness.

58

Such pejorative deformities of sound.
Without meaningful speech or musical equipoise,
Annoyances none but *hoi polloi* enjoys,
Through our winding whispering galleries resound
Unwelcome, & like a tedious siege surround
Us with that ubiquitous nuisance, noise,
Which may take the shape of inflated reputation,
Able neither to stun, astonish nor astound
Those whom obscene publicity annoys,
Who prefer the decent obscurity of publication.

59

Regardless of the weird world's disregard,
These works may be devoted to the wastebasket
Like the forgotten forgeries of some casket
Letters, scored for posterity & scarred
By repentance. Sentenced to a futility of hard
Leisure, answer nothing but the task it
Asks, apart from any eternal return.
Perhaps a masterpiece, unmade, unmarred,
Awaits the patient skill that will unmask it.
A lifetime passes as the phrases turn.

60

Immured in a single-occupancy cell,
Each day indistinguishable from the next,
& nearly inextinguishable, perplexed
How all manner of things shall nevertheless be well,
Will a celibate selfish as a shellfish spell
Out a corrupt & uncorrected text
So that each deleted syllable counts?
Solitude is helpless to dispel
Questions as exceptionably vexed
As unaccountable love's unaudited accounts.

61

To keep your cell the way you keep your soul,
Untidy-minded, neither soiled nor sold
For next to nothing, a treasury of old
Notions like the notes of a piano-roll
Which cannot improvise though it knows a whole
Repertoire, what ought one to withhold?
Idiosyncrasy is nobody else's business.
Of all omens the soul provides the sole
Depository. How many oceans can it hold
In its infinite & unfathomable isness?

62

Sealed & secured, the contents of this room
Turned our intimate alcove into a closet
Concealed behind a dirty bookcase: was it
A conservatory or a living room,
This stanza become a catacomb or tomb
That serves as a temporary safe deposit
Vault for your perduring lost & found
Mind, which articulately could presume
To ask of being what could cause it,
A question as unanswerable as profound.

63

Up the steps of imperfection we stumble & stall,
Blind upstarts, our feeble feet astray & unstable,
Panting after perfections we are no more able
To encompass than an imaginative animal.
While some describe the world as round as a ball,
Others maintain that it is flat like a table.
Its shape is immaterial, there like the air.
Better, perhaps, to be sorry than safe after all,
Seeing no security could enable
One to scale unscathed the inexorable stair.

64

It's up to you to choose, but you must choose,
Preordained to regret a route not taken,
Awakening too late to the fatally mistaken
Nature of a wager few refuse,
With all the winnings none is free to use.
Inexcusably the god-forsaken
Confuse the terms of the bargain: on the whole.
What does it profit anyone to lose
Everything, by everyone forsaken,
Only to win his own immortal soul?

65

That iniquitous bargain, once compacted,
Takes effect on the spot. What you have lost
Will not be missed, no matter what the cost,
Till sooner than later repayment is exacted
& you expect retrospectively that you acted
Too fast. The ghastly transaction cannot be crossed
Off as no more than an impious fraud
If you find yourself, with all which you contracted
For, suspecting you have been double-crossed,
Not by the powers of darkness, but by God.

66

Who, meeting his maker in the supermarket,
Could dream he saw the devil in disguise,
Proffering, as a consolation prize
For your worthless soul, the world, & prepared to mark it
Down? Would anyone refuse to market
That moth-eaten, mythopoeic merchandise?
Although Lucifer too has his stigmata,
Incandescent, open to remark, it
Seems that all too few can recognize
The divine mind underlying his bogus data.

67

All dumb possibilities lost or broken,
Like promises intended to defraud,
Must have begun life ontologically flawed
& now await an off-hand, inaudibly spoken
Spell, the restorative formula in token
Of which some gizmo again becomes a household god.
The tacit history of things mistaken
For totems remains as secret as unspoken
Oracles, inscrutable as odd
Advice unwanted & all too seldom taken.

68

A thingamajig of no particular use
Or immediate interest is dismissed as *it*.
How soon will such a cruel sobriquet befit
The guess-work that you used to introduce,
Without premeditation or excuse,
Into the margin of your narrative bit by bit?
It is not the thing itself but what you make
Of & with it, the marvels you produce
Out of your improvised identikit,
That counts, the shit you reinvented for simplicity's sake.

69

What idiotic, absent-minded soul
Animates this conscious automaton,
Whether well-begun or woebegone,
Programmed to improvise a whole rigmarole
Of autonomic systole & diastole,
Until with & like the dawn it must be gone.
Unless like the dawn it will recur,
Anonymous, to impersonate the role
Of another, forever second-hand & on
Sale—but only one per customer?

70

Who could choose now not to be reborn,
Whether sybaritic on a bed of roses,
The couch where conscience comatose reposes,
Knowing no rose exists without a thorn,
Or more or less unfortunate & forlorn?
Yet among self's myriad metamorphoses
How many endure a lifestyle they never chose?
Absent a night there cannot be a morn.
Opportunity opens before it closes
To disclose no thorn without a rose.

71

Paralytic on no bed of roses,
One supposes no rose exists without a thorn,
Though every night presupposes a better morn.
The restless daybed on which night reposes
& day uncomfortably dozes
Is made up of the tattered & outworn
Habits of a lifetime, carelessly culled & chosen,
That make one wish one never had been born.
Among all of history's histrionic poses,
Many are cold, some permanently frozen.

72

Whenever a thorn is nothing but a thorn,
& there occurs no opening but closes,
So every opportunity life proposes
Seems too hopelessly foolish & forlorn
& the furniture of a lifetime looks shabby & torn,
The presumption of failure then imposes
Regret for another persona than one chose.
Then what choice has anyone but to be reborn
To celebrate the thorns among the roses?
If only there were no thorn without a rose!

73

A rose by another name arose: sore Eros,
The plague that lay bordellos & boarding-schools waste,
Childish, chidden, chastised, yet still unchaste,
Short-sighted as an enraged rhinoceros
Whose impetuous impetus will not spare us
The recycled rejects that we late embraced.
Nor can they escape who take care of themselves
In this perpetual travesty of errors
Whose outcome leaves a tepid aftertaste.
Are we all the reincarnations of ourselves?

74

The question of which the inquisitor insisted
On making his victim an irresistible gift
Persists: why not lackadaisically drift
Amiss through existence, wishing it never existed,
Like a little fishing skiff across some misted
River or lake, disoriented & adrift,
Predicting no landfall's precipitate apparition,
Till the twisted shipwreck of wishes resisted
Pinpoints, as the pitiless mist begins to lift,
Nowhere as its approximate position.

75

Knight errant or errand boy, what naiveté
Misled you through the wordy wilderness,
Where mediocrity in modern dress
Anachronistic as a negligée,
Parades as if the past, because *passé*,
Remained a solecism to suppress,
Till every out of date neologism
Becomes in time a fossilized cliché?
Such errors will tempt the unwary to digress
Into the heresy that created a great schism.

76

What one creates another criticizes,
Whose business is forever to find fault
With everything from the height of heaven's vault
To the procedure at the ultimate assizes:
To the evidence a prosecutor prizes
The defense pretends to prefer a grain of salt.
While your wily adversary may seem a traitor
To the truth with its disguises & surprises,
Victory will be decided by default.
For where would a critic be but for a creator?

77

One survives oneself surprised, today begun,
Already unprepossessing yet unique,
Always in the middle of the three-day week
Of yesterday, today & tomorrow—all anyone
Is immediately aware of, since the sun,
Even when obfuscated or oblique,
Which arose in triumph will subside in sorrow.
As air is the heir of the air, the sun is the son
Of the sun. However brief, the interval seems bleak
Between you yesterday & who but you tomorrow.

78

Only nominally astronomical,
Owing nothing to the phases of the moon
Or the solar year or solar afternoon.
As it recapitulates a biblical
Creation fanatically fantastical,
Unlike the natural calendar's night or noon,
Each day equally memorable & unique
Until name days become numerical,
Interminable or over all too soon:
An arbitrary, ordinary week.

79

In the midst of the abbreviated week
Whose invariable tedium
Circumscribes the maximum & minimum
Limits of our experience, so to speak,
It is one's love that makes one's love unique.
Each love anticipates the love to come
As the sum of that gone by & that just now begun,
All self-contained but pervious enough to leak
Into one another & sometimes become,
Under some specious eternity, only one.

80

Although the secular calendar terms Sunday
The first day of the nonsabbatarian week,
Those know otherwise for whom the bleak
Workaday week begins with Monday,
A tiresome, reluctantly begun day,
Inevitable, shabby & unchic.
Despite the peculiarities of choice,
Chance will disillusion everyone day
By day. Retrospectively all days speak
With the same inimitable voice.

81

In the grip of an eternal interdenominational Sunday,
A rag-bag knitted by the nonsectarian sun,
When winter soon will see its dirty work undone,
Just such another clumsily homespun day,
That rerun day introductory to Monday,
As tacky & predictable as downtown Evanston,
Of all the days with which one was entrusted,
One could only hope this notoriously no fun day,
Would turn out to be the ultimate one
On which, in the words of *Genesis*, "God rusted".

82

This atypical day defines an intemperate zone
Whose sun reflects the gaudy sun in vain
From icy pond & blinded windowpane,
Frozen foliage & stippled stone,
Old undergrowth cold frost has overgrown,
To spread a distempered indiscriminate stain
Over every other undistinguished thing.
Though never less alone than when alone,
Not even to oneself can one explain,
The shapes the stereotypical shadows bring.

83

Ever more flamboyant after sunset,
In the battlemented West a bonfire burned,
Once all unhappy returns had been returned.
One has seen too many suns & every one set
Sooner or later; each day abruptly begun set
Unperturbed, like linen curtains furled & turned
Inside out so their lineaments reflected
The colours of the wind. Before the sun set
One learned the contours of a hardly earned
Certain love returned & not rejected.

84

Touch wood! Would I were not so superstitious
& my incredulity less abject,
With fewer suspicious objects to object
To, no dates & numbers so unpropitious
As to vitiate the reasonable wishes
Of the irrationally circumspect!
Religion's ineradicable rival,
Inexplicable, primitive & all too auspicious
Collective superstitions recollect
Nothing more silly or sinister than survival.

85

To get through it you must go to the other side.
There are no detours or shortcuts in the soul,
No shady companionships with which to console
Oneself, nor shabby habitations in which to hide,
Only a no-man's land almost as wide
& perilous & unwholesome as the whole
World, although its ways are not the same,
A loveless suburb where love continues to reside.
The soul alone can reanimate the sole
Self-same soul that does not even have a name.

86

Do you suppose it will go on forever,
When nothing lasts, not even suffering.
Not even death, not even everything?
The future, an impracticable endeavour,
Presents few empty menaces however,
No promissory notes, considering
A bankrupt, implacable, blackmailing past
That seemed too temporary. Never ever
Ask that inconvenient guest to bring
With it anything too implausible to last.

87

Staggering backwards down the spectral stair,
After an infinite number of false alarms.
Expecting to be caught up in nobody's arms,
You stumble, half awake, not unaware
Of the missing step, a palisade of air
& the echoing chasm's uncanny charms,
To grasp a nonexistent banister, then drop
Through vacant space where there is nothing there
But emptiness, which disarms before it harms,
In a free fall that unlike time will never stop.

88

Sanity swings on medicated hinges
In momentary danger of coming unhinged
When premedicated memory, which cringed
Undercover in anaesthetic binges,
Unreasonable as a mechanism impinges
On territories sorely scorched or psychically singed.
The Great God Pain conducts his night campaign
Amid suppositories & syringes
With mortality indelicately tinged,
Leaving his victims temporarily insane.

89

What if the future were a wish-fulfillment?
Who can be sure which wishes would come true?
Take care of yourself & your self will take care of you,
When might becomes may, & all your silly, ill-meant
Resolutions, including the few that still meant
Something to you, must willy-nilly be carried through.
When faith is a drug & hope a placebo, what
Of those disillusionments that, say what you will, meant
Take care of the day & the day will take care of you?
Tomorrow will offer all that yesterday did not.

90

Confused as the labyrinth none issues from,
As repetitive, self-centred yet diffuse,
A sole survivor labours to reproduce
Some narrative incredible as some
Taradiddle to illustrate the tedium
Of humdrum humiliation & abuse,
Hoping the tolerant light of day will salve
Memory's mediocre medium,
Which accepts oblivion as no excuse:
Today is not much but it is all we have.

91

When does your diary become a journal?
When you have something commonplace to say
Or write beyond the ephemeral everyday.
Between the temporary & the eternal,
Betwixt the heavenly & the infernal,
Exists a compromise, a middle way:
Neither/nor, no longer, or not yet.
Yet among all the dreary, difficult & diurnal
Details circumstantial as today,
It is the significant one one will forget.

92

What could be more forgettable than the present
Unless it is remembered as the past?
No last act was ever meant to last,
However valedictory & unpleasant.
Your present remains a soon forgotten present
Like a pleasant morning presently overcast
To which a few evanescent impressions cling,
A moment temporarily unsurpassed.
Nevertheless the past seems omnipresent
As a vernal Fall or an autumnal Spring.

93

Like the repetition of the seasons
All but everything comes back again,
Surprising pleasure & astounding pain.
Besides the spice, variety, that seasons
The trite predictability of reason's
Reiterated rhymes, the same refrain
Underlies or overlays creation
Despite the devolution of such unreasons
As the reasonable alone may entertain,
A paradox whose theme is variation.

94

Alive to every quaint & crazy feature
Of the future, a newcomer gawked around
At all the rockery & greenery at ground
Level, himself an unprecedented creature
Amidst the other nameless novelties of nature
Whose anonymous anomalies confound
The curiosity with which an expert inspects
The unexpected, measuring his stature
Against such excess. Both sprung from underground,
The fountain overflows, the pond reflects.

95

Lost in a pocketty landscape a fraudulent pool
Was by a poculent hollow frondescently cupped;
Drawn, at what cost, a wanderer stopped, stooped & supped
From the mercurial surface his own superficially cool
Image, through which an elementary school
Of minnows flickered, too minimal to disrupt
His auto-intoxication. The looking-glass glistened,
Enraptured at having captivated a natural fool
Who fell for himself. Nothing else could interrupt
The echo to which this narcissist hardly listened.

96

What if the soul were like a pond, transparent
As a window, yet a little murky.
Beyond the pond life, fronds & fish as perky
As foolish notions, the bottom lies apparent,
Fond & fundamental as a parent,
All too often questionable & quirky.
Yet what is a pool when you come down to it but a hole
In the ground which, filled by underground inerrant
Watery currents, furnishes a sure key
To what for want of another word we call the soul.

97

Beside the fountainhead to die of thirst,
By the fireside to perish of the cold,
So long as fire & water will withhold
Their elementary blessings from a cursed
Tantalus whose need, so long rehearsed,
Is too obvious to need to be retold,
Appears as unnecessary now as what
Was wanted; nor is second best the worst
Of worlds. Somehow to have & not to hold
May seem impossible, but what was not?

98

The material subject of the world, unvaried,
For all its multiplicity the same,
Besides the so-called self that has no name
Whose variegated pseudonyms miscarried
As its substance never materially varied
From an anonymous, extinguishable flame,
Answers an enigma with a riddle:
What we are engaged with, but never married
To, remains more than a language game,
With no beginning but an interminable middle.

99

Except for an immaculate deception,
A little self-knowledge is a dubious thing.
The same thing might be said for suffering
Unmitigated by the misperception
Of pain as an inexplicable exception
Such as any unexpected day can bring
To the least exceptional existence;
Innocuous as it may seem in its inception,
One soon will lose perspective, till everything
Diminishes in proportion to its distance.

100

Distances indelicately dissembling
Deliberate differences keep
Us distinct, unless perhaps sometimes in sleep
Where we collude, forever reassembling
Disparate dreams, dazed, diffident & trembling,
Yet never more awake than when asleep,
Each the indifferent idol we adore,
One another eerily resembling.
As dissent seemed easy so assent seems steep,
Till I become a window, you a door.

101

Polluting alike the pleasant & the plain—
Its epicentre neither here nor there
For long, confounding nowhere with anywhere—
Emotive & unemotional squalls the rain,
Of which it would be stupid to complain
As if it encompassed nothing beyond compare
With the weather's incurable misbehaviour,
Nor any watertight system to explain
The unpredictable movements of the air,
Our omnipresent, necessary saviour.

102

Ageless, remote from every human woe,
This superannuated superman,
Unconsciously a god, self-consciously a man,
Expired on a pyre an age ago,
Whose incandescent instant, still aglow,
Marks the moment when his myth began
Its afterlife. A mortal, though no more
Aware of the heroic lapse of time, once slow
Now faster than an average life-span,
Must find immortality a bore.

103

Fools ourselves, we think by fooling others
To fool ourselves & thereby circumvent
That guilt whose extent declares one innocent.
Born of indifferent fathers & different mothers,
All men, who ought to be but are not brothers,
Confront an identical predicament:
Forever fretful & everywhere in fetters,
Each questions his reflection in another's
Intense, incomprehensible intent.
Forgiven our bets, can we forgive our betters?

104

Some murmurous rain relieves the siege of summer.
Meanwhile a soggy equinox precesses
& leaf by leaf each embarrassed tree undresses,
Yet the insect chorus grows no dumber
Than during out-door concerts in midsummer
When the wood was an underworld of wildernesses.
As the years accelerate, the seasons creep
Along, each like some lackadaisical latecomer,
All in low-cut, unfashionable dresses.
It is not beauty but the woods that sleep.

105

Still up in the air though earthbound, undecided
As the weather, whether dry & cold
Or warm & humid, golden oldies hold
Barely to the luxuriance summer prided
Itself on, which autumn soon will have elided,
Foliage mutlicoloured, manifold.
A fall as ambiguous as the equinox
When night & day are equally divided,
That time of year you may in time behold
When we must soon be putting back the clocks.

106

An arid August brought these wet September
Days abbreviated as well as wetter,
Small alterations in ephemeral weather
No one is expected to remember.
The sun that yesterday glared like an ember
Hovers today obsequious as a waiter
Faintly supercilious overhead.
The club which everybody is a member
Of has got a not-forgotten motto: water
Is the stuff of life instead of bread.

107

Overnight the temperature dropped
Below the freezing mark as leaves let go
Their grip on life, whose juices ceased to flow
When the affluence of summer stopped.
Soon the august mountains will be topped
Again with powdered periwigs of snow
As migratory music fills the sky,
The overture of a show that never flopped
Throughout its extended run a year ago.
This is the equinox, & Fall is passing by.

108

Are leaves, discoloured brown & red & gold,
So called because they must at last take leave
Of naked limbs they cannot hope to cleave
To forever, till separated by the cold,
As if shivering at the propinquity of old
Age & losses time will not relieve.
That pathetic fallacy will not outlast
Our facile sympathy, when leaves unfold
A lassitude we would rather disbelieve
Until surpassed, alas, by a last 'At last!'

109

Nowadays the exponential rate
Of loss has accelerated overnight,
In face of a dawn triumphant yet as trite
As sunset, & as second-rate,
As if its lateness might exaggerate
The latent possibilities of light
As everyday hyperbole or hype.
Sometimes it seems unrighteous not to wait
For recognition of a recondite
Stone cliché or buried archetype.

110

Most clichés conceal a metaphor,
Though not all metaphors contain clichés.
Stale insights with a hackneyed turn of phrase
Enjoy a short shelf-life before they bore
Us like a tragic chorus: less is more
More or less, not least in paraphrase.
If the light at the end of the tunnel is a sign
Of an oncoming locomotive, or
The end of the line, the end of all holidays,
What sea-change will define our bottom line?

111

Comfortable words come as some reassurance,
Like long-standing habits & an ideal temperature,
In the face of the unfamiliar, to reassure
With illusions of security. Recurrence
Amid chaotic cross-&-undercurrents,
While making one temporarily secure,
Subversively exacts a certain cost.
Sturdy enough to endure her own endurance,
Even nervous Nature never can be sure
When the borderline of comfort has been crossed.

112

You need not ask permission of the clock
Whose imaginary, arbitrary chimes,
Synchronizing meals with set mealtimes
& sleep with bedtime, sometimes seem to mock
Everyday existence with a baroque
Timetable preordained to table time's
Inchoate oceanic swell,
Till the clock's inexorable tic-toc
Stops, & afterthought in echo rhymes
Other past times with other pastimes as well.

113

It ever was too late for vain regret
Or wonders that will never come again,
But after all not all regrets are vain,
Unless for that which has not happened yet,
Which one is yet unable to forget:
Precipitous & soppy as the rain
Along a long & melancholy road
Where drip-dry branches made the windshield wet,
Happiness in a narrative of pain
Ranks as an exceptional episode.

114

History as landscape may explain,
Our ups & downs & dangerous interchanges,
How intransigent, monarchic mountain ranges
Dominate the democratic plain,
The egalitarian, flat champaign.
As earth subsides, the immutable sea changes
Forever, for the heavens never rest,
While reigns as transitory as the rain
Fall & rise. Each successive regime arranges
Fresh perspectives, new points of interest.

115

Amid twisty thickets of hidden indecision
In which penultimate decisions hide,
Besides an inability to decide,
A dim vision of dismal imprecision,
Resides a certain element of derision.
Sometimes the straightest by-way will divide
The path to Athens & the track to Sparta,
The gated community & the subdivision.
We must abide by what we would deride,
Our own pragmatic, unratified Magna Carta.

116

Although you had the soul of Superman,
With the spirit to engage in flighty word-play,
& were able to imitate a bird, play
What airs you like on any instrument you can
Command in language far from spick-&-span
that will not scan, you, I have heard, play
Fast & loose with figurative & abstract
Variations, who in fact began
As the antagonist in an absurd play
Enacted off-stage in the *entr'actes*.

117

Afterwards, when the first psychodrama
Seemed ended, its protagonist popped up again,
Blinded by belated recognition. Then
At the catastrophe of our paradigmatic drama,
Amid some periphrastic, questionable grammar,
The chorus croaked, *Alas for the affairs of mortal men*!
Predictable as the dénouement of the play,
The scene dissolved, resolved. The cyclorama
Revolved. Aghast, the same old gentlemen
Grumbled, *Such have been the doings of today*.

118

Why try to extemporize a dry Attic
Tragedy for barbarians who speak
Not one unaccented syllable of Greek
In choruses spontaneous yet static
Whose uneven lines end in emphatic
Agreement even when the cases are oblique,
Like the predatory & degenerative?
Happy the man who, asymptomatic,
Never had to memorize the days of the weak
&, forgiven, knows of nothing to forgive.

119

Metanoia: when & if you change your mind
May involve an instantaneous change of heart.
In light of the ambiguities of art,
Indecision chronically ill-defined
Defines the new uncertainties we find,
Apart from the dogmas we are sad to part
With. Inconsistency, the shibboleth of small
Minds, means we never finish where we start.
What disbelief dictated blind faith signed;
Witness the spurious conversion of Saint Paul.

120

The morning my dear antagonist up & vanished
Dawned predictably mysterious
Enough to worry us & weary us:
The milky carafe of early light replenished,
& the world as bright as woodwork newly varnished.
In the event that he was serious
& will turn out to have gone away for good,
Thoughts of his return were better banished
Whose dereliction proved so deleterious.
If you would not when you may, you could not when
        you would.

121

Catastrophes occur often with no warning;
Disaster hits you right between the eyes.
But happiness too may happen by surprise
When to an ineluctable night of mourning
Succeeds at last the inevitable morning
& a clarity no cloud-cover can disguise,
As if each moment were a monument
With a particular epigraph adorning
It that signifies what could not be otherwise:
Not every happening qualifies as an event.

122

Satisfaction, imperfect anywhere you find
It, lacks the sophistication of afterthought,
Like the upshot of some overcomplicated plot
Left behind by the mastermind who designed
It as his masterpiece, but never signed
It, dissatisfied—or possibly he forgot
All that was lost, like a ghost or a gust of wind. O
If time were a watch & you forgot to wind
It, would it stop eventually? Maybe not?
What waltzed in the door will flit back out the window.

123

The shy violet & the brazen pansy must
Wither & wilt whether or never plucked;
Even artificial constructs self-destruct
When their silky, metallic petals rust,
Indestructible as they are robust.
After such florid arrangements have been tucked
Away, the day will betray the glamour of the hour
Whose fragmented, anthological lust
Its fragrance proves too frail to reconstruct,
As the fruit frustrates the promise of the flower.

124

Inherent not only in the squint of the beholder,
Beauty seems painfully self-evident.
As an extraordinary event,
It stands out like an error, only bolder.
Reputations tarnish, idols moulder,
& perfection is in itself impermanent.
Physical attractions cannot last
Once their potency grows a moment older.
As soon as enthusiasm is misspent
Every aesthete becomes an iconoclast.

125

Misrepresenting whatever nature made,
Art artfully transmogrifies, or will
Mistranslate innate, incarnate chlorophyll
Into amethyst, quartz, cornelian & jade,
Translucent foliage displayed
Ostentatiously on my windowsill.
The charms of such hard-hearted artistry
Shown in the shade of this semi-precious mineral glade
Will hardly fool & nor yet fully fill
The place of an all but artificial tree.

126

Yard, which is a metonym for garden,
Also stands for the hardy organ of regeneration,
This rigid effigy; by implication
What is a garden god without a hard-on,
A garlanded warden to mount lusty guard on
An orchard, his traditional station?
When the West wind whispers an indelicate suggestion,
Dropping hints to make Priapus harden
As a vegetable emblem of procreation,
Would he? Will he? What a ridiculous question!

127

This fallacious symbol will still persist
Down the garden, within the garden gate,
With ivory crowned & hornbeam implicate,
Where undergrowth & hardwoods coexist,
Stuck stark upright, a sturdy animist
Image of an uncomplicated state,
Commonplace & not too hard to comprehend,
Whose indelicate decency does not desist
Whenever chiliasts anticipate
Some millennium. This world will never end.

128

Yesterday the sun came up again
After an excruciating night,
To scour with indiscriminate appetite
The grown-up mountains & pubescent plain,
Its light not quite sufficient to explain
The shadows undeveloped overnight.
What illumination will ever be enough
To eliminate every unsightly nightly stain
Of sorrow indispensable to delight,
With all that other incriminating stuff?

129

The steady crepitation of the rain
Awoke me in the middle of the night
With its inane dactyloepitrite
Off-beat, as half asleep in some insane
Dream I lay beneath the counterpane,
Listening for silence to alight.
Thus irrigated, spring need not regret
The patter song that on the windowpane
Spells out the evidence that overnight
This world will have gone from white on white to wet.

130

That solvent gaze, those silver eyes that kept
A tremulous teardrop pendant on a lash on
Lustrous cheeks still glistening with passion
Taught me to weep because another wept.
Dry-eyed I watched beside you while you slept
Rapt in such defeats as dreams can fashion,
With the night sky over & the light earth under,
A manuscript illegible except
Where punctuated by compassion,
Written in tears to be reread in wonder.

131

Having lost your mind, why keep on looking for
It high & low? Identity inheres
In the inheritance of months & years
That is private property. To explore,
Or more or less authentically restore
It, will take time, & time of course costs tears.
Its former glories forsaken & unwanted
As a sand castle abandoned on the shore,
Abridged with sighs, awash with souvenirs,
It lies in ruins though the site is haunted.

132

An exile who had everything to forget
& more to remember than he could afford
To, returned to an implausibly restored
Ruin, by irrepressible regret
For unforgettable foolishness beset.
There the records of felicity were stored
Away, indexed under dirt & ash,
A few asbestos embers igneous yet,
Less easily extinguished than ignored,
& treasures indistinguishable from trash.

133

For ages now with nowhere to reside,
My home wrecked, & no one to repair it,
I summed up my despair & tried to square it:
But nothing when by nothing multiplied
Comes to nothing. How then can I decide
On some temporary residence or who to share it—
Who being of course an anagram for *how*
Much my misery might be magnified
To instruct me in solitude & how to bear it,
Homeless but not quite hopeless anyhow.

134

Hotel & hospital stem from the same root-word
As hospitality, which meant both *host* & *guest*.
Such radical affinities suggest
A certain reciprocity inferred
Between inhabitants hospitably immured,
Despite a mutual lack of interest.
This world is an hotel or hospital,
A sinecure where nobody is cured,
A rest room where nobody comes to rest,
& a home where no one is at home at all.

135

Awakened by two incompatible voices
Next door, distorted by propinquity, enraged,
Which in the middle of the silly night engaged
In too audible debate—as one weeps one rejoices
Contrapuntally over ridiculous choices.
While they ranted, recriminated & rampaged,
I tried to intermit them with a cough,
Ignored amid unforgiven debts & overdue invoices:
A disagreeable performance perhaps for my sake staged?
Or had they forgotten to turn the t.v. off?

136

Absent some immaculate conception,
Were it cosier not to have been conceived at all
Than born in this inhospitable hospital?
In lieu of the miracle of contraception,
To which our very existence proves an exception,
Who could prevent the consequences that the Fall
Fatally frustrated before it had begun?
Howbeit subject to prior misconception,
Consider this concept unexceptional:
Death & conception in mankind are one.

137

Born in this seraglio, I know its ins & outs
Inside out, by heart & hearing, sight & scent & touch,
Yet its errors terrorize me, inasmuch
As theirs is the treacherous evidence no one doubts
In distinguishing the centre's whereabouts
From the windings of the labyrinth where such
Exits as look like entrances appear no nearer—
Through the byways & the roundabouts
Which are always with & within us all too much—
Than the dead ends that confront us in the mirror.

138

In this hotel (nor are we out of it)
Shelter such perambulatory shades
As intolerable age that masquerades
As useless youth, whose features do not befit
Facades disintegrating bit by bit,
Which would trade their hand-me-downs for ready-mades,
Hell's antechambers no one becomes inured
To, the pitiless bottom of the bottomless pit,
Infernal neverlands & eternal everglades:
What cannot be enjoyed must be endured.

139

This decrepit hostelry, my down-at-heels Bastille,
Uninhabited by the uninhibited spirit of de Sade
Who, determined to be rather bad than sad,
Could care less what others feel or that they feel
At all, unconvinced that anyone else is real,
Incarnates the most radical, perverse ideal he had:
That pain, not just a displeasing sensation to avoid
Or transcend, or to ignore, pretending it is unreal,
Must be so suffered that suffering may be, although so bad
It cannot be cured, not just endured but enjoyed.

140

On another such negligible morning,
Staring out & away beyond the fire-escape
Of the staid hotel I stayed in, on a cityscape
Prettified by the smut & smoke adorning
It, despicable but not therefore worth scorning,
As insubstantial as if made of crepe,
I thought of the indefinable beyond & yawned.
Too early for an epiphany, too late for a warning,
The nugatory details of today took shape,
As forgettable a day as never dawned.

141

For what need one accept no substitute
But existence? Ostensibly a crime
Against oneself is neither victimless nor a sublime
Victory (from the same vindictive root
As *victim* & *vigour*) nor yet an absolute
Solution to the tyranny of time.
Bored by the book of life & its perusal,
Sick of the seed, fed up with the fruit,
As with the exigencies of reason, ditto rhyme,
One contemplates no ultimate refusal.

142

Whatever whatever method may recover,
Some sense of the past but never the scent of it,
Not even the least significant tidbit
Of something sensible can reverie discover.
All the rest, veiled, unavailable, undercover,
Remain as reminders of what time will not remit,
Unless rhymes, themselves memories, like such reminders
As a face or a fragrance might restore a lover
Momentarily, turning a key that few locks fit:
Losers weepers, but keepers must first be finders.

143

As yesterday demanded another hand-out
I wondered, when would enough not be enough?
Yes, times are tough, but time was always tough,
& while none of our long-term speculations panned out,
Why should one mediocre failure stand out
From all the rest? Through seldom smooth & all too
         often rough
Pathologies we huffed & puffed. Now it's time to part.
Still there the past stands with an exacting hand out,
Nor even thanks one for such nonnegotiable stuff
As indulgence in life that finds no place in art.

144

Empathetic in their tatterdemalion pride,
Through a deceptive accidental screen
Indistinctly deciduous, can be seen
Two nonagenarian oak trees side by side,
The leaves of one discoloured, dead & dried
Up already, the other's foliage still green.
Notwithstanding their contemporaneity, each tree
At a different rate has superficially died,
Until this one's limbs, stripped bare & clean,
Only emphasize the other's clinging, lingering greenery.

145

Recollected in senility, how forgive
One's own selectively elected sins?
The forgiveness an obstinate recidivist wins
From himself must eventually give
Way to a criminal nature forced to live
Wherever individuality begins.
We cannot lie before we learn to speak
Half-truths we truly are reduced to relive.
For all the falsehoods a romancer spins,
The truth it is that makes no lie unique.

146

Faced with anything but alternatives,
A heretic left with nothing to retract—
All tricks tried, chiasmus, equivocal tact,
Tactful equivocation—rhetorically forgives
The just unjust as controversy gives
Up. No incident, no episode, but an act
Of faith fuelled this incontrovertible burning.
Like the kingdom of heaven justice lives
Forever, not without us, as a fact,
But within us as an unappeasable yearning.

147

Another milestone, & another millstone
Is added to any attempt to recollect
More than one was ever able to collect.
An effigy representative, yet still stone,
Its perfection petrified until stone
Reverts to flesh in treasured retrospect,
That lodestone affects affection like a magnet,
Attracting everyone against their will, stone
Being all that anybody can expect
From anything dredged up in memory's dragnet.

148

At the antepenultimate instant instinct swerved
Away from all but inevitable danger,
With the sleights of hand of an adept shape-changer,
& a presence of mind too dexterous to be observed.
As if by a mere mistake momentarily unnerved,
At each near escape from any musical arranger
Who would affront me with an improved, alternative version,
So far my conservative impulse has preserved
Me from the attentions of that persistent stranger
For whom I felt an instantaneous aversion.

149

Night after night *L'Elissir d'Amore*
Failed to come off: long before the discredits rolled.
Interest flickered at the same old antics served up cold,
A stale, stereotypical bedtime story,
Neither a parable nor an allegory
But the facts of life compulsively retold
As fictions, wherein incidentally one discerns
Amid resourceful, shameless, sore & sorry
Beauties almost too breath-taking to behold,
The law of eternally diminishing returns.

150

Nobodies with abbreviated names,
Objects of deplorable desire,
Lissome, writhe & wither in the fire,
Licked by lubricious tongues of wicked flames,
Self-satisfied in their forbidden games,
Admirable but risky to admire.
It is their own enjoyment one enjoys,
A *joie de vivre* no disappointment tames
Until they are committed to the pyre,
Combustible as once & only paper boys.

151

After prime time everything repeats
In reruns of reversible disaster,
As predictable mishaps follow ever faster
Amid misunderstandings & deceits,
Till a plastic protagonist defeats
A virtual antagonist of plaster.
If life were like a sitcom, it might envision
The trials of grace & will, where each competes
As to which will prove the momentary master.
So old age mimics late night television.

152

As an exemplary maverick, Alexander
Laid waste everything in sight & died of drink,
Chagrined at the edge of unknown worlds to think
There were no conquests left, no grandeur grander
Than his grand-standing, though as a bystander
He wept to watch the limits of ignorance shrink.
Like even this "most excellent of men",
Through a land of ruins we used to meander
Over mountains of paper & rivulets of ink,
When then was now. Now will too soon be then.

153

Those who have power to hurt but none to harm,
Unlike many maniacal movers & shakers,
Prime time wasters, & unfunny moneymakers,
Prove, in practice, pretty difficult to disarm.
The insidious guile & invidious charm
Of such as were never givers & ever takers
Can all but obliterate indifference.
We welcome with open arms, not without alarm,
Those irresistible homewreckers & heartbreakers
Who define the line between innocence & experience.

154

The Latin canon gabbled backwards, the sign
Of the cross upside down, an idolized phallus
On the altar where a defrocked priest sips from a chalice
Of disgusting, transubstantiated wine:
What belief is implicit in this malign design!
There surely are no sceptical or callous
Assistants at a blasphemous black mass
Where sacred verses vice versa redefine
The true faith, while a theatrical malice
Laughs behind the Satanic looking-glass.

155

Inspiration anywhere we look?
Perhaps, but all too often we are blind.
In appearances or all that lies behind
Them or, surreptitiously in a book,
There is so much we cannot help but overlook
Which we will recognize not when we find
It, but when it finds us. It must speak up first,
Even a will-o'-the-wisp which one mistook
With that most fallible of instruments, the mind,
For a break-through, outrageous & unrehearsed.

156

Trite, trivial, troublesome, untruthfulness
Must have originated with the word
As pure reference, whereby nothing was referred
To yet, a wrong too implausible to redress.
Seeing the truth undressed, we hasten to re-dress
It, by simple shamelessness undeterred,
Since if one could bare it one could barely bear it?
Better an over-dressed No than a naked Yes.
Though disbelieving, who has ever heard
A lie that was entirely without merit?

157

What if the whole truth were nothing but a lie,
An invention or perhaps a perversion,
Or merely, & not so merely, another version
Of the certitude it was created by?
Would that not provide an inadequate pretext why
Simpleminded animadversion
Fastened not on a single thread but a tangled strand,
Like clouds against a fabricated sky
Of truth, which provokes such universal aversion:
Etc., &, ampersand, and per se and.

158

In that unhappy valley before the rift
Opened into a chasm where no rope
Offered a handhold for fantasy & hope
Across an abyss so precipitously cliffed
By all the evidence of sentimental drift
That faith passed for a habit, love for a trite trope,
An emotional alpinist learned how to cope with his
Extraordinary, unappreciated gift,
Although prone perhaps to exaggerate its scope.
If a man be not his own audience, who is?

159

At the end of all days darkness comprehended
A presence that no longer had a name,
As its various beauties bit by bit became
Hardly the effigy daylight had befriended,
So specific, specialized & splendid,
Yet underneath & after all the same
Over-painted, somber masterpiece.
When at last the indecisive twilight ended
In disbelief & blasphemy & blame,
Even the blackest, bleakest sorrow might find a kind of peace.

160

One of these days will be one of those days
When unhappiness happens as it has done
Already, & an anonymous anyone
Wonders what calendar could disclose days
So unspeakable: surely no omen chose days
On which no one could hope to see the sun?
Open this envelope: a stanza, an enclosure
Of dated prose, days-old frivolities that froze days
Ago, both overwrought & underdone,
All subject to evening's closure & disclosure.

161

So why not let the sun set on your sorrow?
Soon the macabre scene will be growing dim
With the approach of shadowy visitors like grim
Regret, & the wish to repudiate tomorrow.
Let the bankrupt, shabby future borrow
Its ration of anguish from its antonym,
The past, which afforded occasion enough to grieve,
& darkness unconditional & thorough,
A medium in which melancholy monsters swim
From night till day, from dawn to dewy eve.

162

Somewhere a splendour never without setting,
Not yet exhausted, although somewhat overwrought,
Will have settled down on some enlightened spot,
A future-perfect sunset perennially upsetting.
Elsewhere another lazy day is getting
Up, improbably fine, implausibly hot,
Upon morning lands our late evening land lies on
Like a memory forever beyond forgetting.
Nothing will be lost no matter what.
Light radiates from under the horizon.

163

Slow off the mark, Spring, a dispirited sprinter
Boggles & balks, half-hearted & hard to start,
Although given several bleak weeks' head-start,
Its heart anaesthetized by a suppurating splinter
Of ice left over from a stark midwinter.
Starved for the immobility of art,
It stalls & stops like an uncooperative go-cart.
Stuck in this oxymoronic vernal hinter-
Land, we pine for springtime's counterpart,
& live out of the empty icebox of the heart.

164

There must be another way around the boring
Straits, away from the route of the normal horde.
When the whole continental self has been explored,
Any such detour would be well worth exploring,
The whales' highway or the flyway of soaring
Birds, or a fjord no ordinary mortal can afford,
That subaqueous path that used to be dry land,
An ancient road degraded beyond restoring.
The alternatives seem to be bored or overboard,
While each & every continent began as an island.

165

A background annoyance—the song of water flowing
From cataracts & taps that dribble, spurt & spout
The fluid, vivifying substance out,
Repetitive & predictable as plain sewing,
Carelessly, extravagantly bestowing
The sole benediction no body can do without—
Soothes & enchants with the noise of uppity fountains,
Waterways' & waves' compulsive to-ing & fro-ing,
To inform us what recreation was all about.
Rainfall unlike faith, can remove mountains.

166

Willows wept & aspens were wont to quiver
Along a pretty, polluted riverbank;
Stagnant as the Styx, the effluvium stank,
Whose effluent made rank foliage shake & shiver.
Disgusting rubbish flushed away downriver
In the ugly current sluggishly sank.
Each lifetime has a beginning & a muddle
& an end like every living river,
Nor can one often see from bank to bank.
Must the love canal debouch in a mud puddle?

167

The upshot: who would not be shocked
At such a change of status? Cinderella shall
Have exchanged a subservient for the principal
Role, & flirted, laughed & danced & talked
Nonsense as automatically she walked
Like a palindrome backwards, our temporal
Contemporary, down the marble steps of the palace,
Getting home late to find the back door locked,
Her luck unchanged, the joke made flesh, the jovial
House of mirth become the abode of malice.

168

Tomorrow who has never loved will love:
Whoever has loved before will love tomorrow.
Although acquainted, indeed intimate, with sorrow,
You might delight in another light-of-love,
Or, having said no to none of the above,
Find it not impossible to borrow
A part-time partner for the masquerade ball.
Accept the invitation of the morrow
In order to discover whom to be enamoured of:
Better to have loved & lost than never to have lost at all?

169

One who loves anyone, but not everyone,
Will discover that different affections tend
In the optional light of hindsight all to blend,
Transcending trivial comparison,
As The Many dissolve into The One,
In the prototype of an ideal Friend,
Until you scarcely have a thought to spare
For a new edition of your sun
To be reissued, praying that the world will never end
Here & now, no matter how, nor anywhere.

170

These few friendships as far apart appear
As liminal, spectacular events,
Their distance equal to their indifference;
So different constellations disappear
Into nowhere, never to reappear
Light years later, as an acquaintance which represents
An aftermath with no hereafter,
While the dead approach, so diffident, so dear,
Ignorant of any but the perfect tense,
As if present grief brought everlasting laughter.

171

Branches, already getting buddy-buddy,
Wave through the window's distinguished opening
To signal a radical annual happening
When almost any body (or anybody)
May raise again their bowed but seldom bloody
Morning standards as hangers-on of the Spring,
Flattering, precocious & thin-skinned,
Hopefully, as bed-ridden shut-ins study
Flimsy curtains whose flibbertigibbet fluttering
Informs the coloured contours of the wind.

172

Transparent as this limpid element,
Its errant streams that from some fountainhead
Through watery mazes mazy waters spread
In indolent ways that lazily came & went.
Semantic was the original event
That marked the deliquescent watershed,
A beverage from liquid pearls distilled.
Never may this perpetual spring be spent,
But brim with fluent sentences, instead,
From a reservoir eternally refilled!

173

Nowadays & overnight the rate
Of loss has gone up exponentially,
Illustrating the redundancy
(All too soon before it is too late)
Of that which abstraction will exaggerate—
Present distress & past felicity,
Irrespective of a domestic holocaust.
Sometimes it is impossible to wait
For that ultimate calamity
When not only paradise is lost.

174

When shall we learn what must be clear as mud:
We are not free to choose, or not to choose,
The love we like & are too like to lose?
The alchemy embodied in the blood,
Like a blossom implicit in a bud,
Infuses a home brew useless to refuse
For all its bitterly insipid aftertaste.
Yet the desert will recover from the flood
An arid parterre of florid tints & hues:
Not even the wasteland ever goes to waste.

175

A force notorious for breaking eggs
& not making omelets, under all the nicknames for
Her, a metonym that is no metaphor,
Nature not unnaturally never begs
Pardon for the principles she reneges
On, whether you adore her or deplore.
Sempiternal nearly, or merely chronic,
One cannot contradict, counterfeit or ignore
Her, but must drink her bitter elixir to the dregs,
When what's-her-face brews up her nauseous spring tonic.

176

In the Sign of the Ram underpants grow hairy
Amid rampant outbreaks of satyriasis,
Battening now on that & now on this
Involuntary voluptuary
Whom appetite has driven to the very
Brink of the blankety-blank, blissed-out abyss,
Where all intimate acquaintances seem quaint.
In view of a few extraordinary
Scenes, where a chaste caress becomes an obscene kiss,
Is there more to any painting than the paint?

177

Were we nothing but coincidences,
Chemical, genetic accidents
Under the palimpsest of experience,
What would one want with pregnable defenses,
Permeable walls & undependable senses
To become not independent persons but events,
As in *Du bist der Lenz*? This bleary Spring will teach
Us, with its horticultural experiments,
Indefensible fences & expendable expenses,
What it meant to be out of touch yet not out of reach.

178

Sentenced to an eternity of unsatisfactory labour,
I foresaw my *Works & Days* forgotten in the waste
Basket, *Theogony*—& the ecstasy—misbegotten & disgraced,
But morning after morning I continue to belabour
The word horde with its resources of *gai saber,*
Until the understated stalemate leaves an aftertaste
Of triumph or defeat, & maybe a promise of revenge
Against some ill-favoured, imaginary neighbour.
Endless work erases nothing, like that never-to-be replaced
Neolithic chronometer, Stonehenge.

179

Remainders, reminders, slanted to make one wonder
At their odd inclinations, how sloppily they slope
Away from or towards each other, as if in hope
Or aversion; barely able to stay asunder,
They have measured innumerable suns, which under
Standing stones compose a motionless heliotrope
Calendar, where uncounted months & moments tumble
Over & over headlong as centuries blunder
Through the anhistorical horrors of the horoscope,
Until these meaningless prehistoric memorials crumble.

180

No recognition of necessity revokes
The categorical imperative. *Ought* & *should*
Must invoke some absolute, peremptory good
Half understood, whose injunctions most of us treat as jokes,
But which form the hub of which we all are the spokes.
The wheel of the will constructed out of *would*
Would wobble, were its purpose not so steady.
The cauldron bubbles & the tripod smokes,
The statues are standing where they always stood,
Strait is the gate, & you are through already.

181

If life is vulgar, what distinguished thing,
Otherwise unmentionable, were not?
Who would not prefer a jolly polyglot
Slang to a language too uptight to say anything?
Or the tawdry trinkets that the senses bring
To the rotten tributes posterity ought to have brought?
Or mortal vitality to a marmoreal *rigor*
Mortis? The rude exuberance of spring
To frigid perfection? Ribaldry to rot?
& to the promise of extinction a remembered vigour?

182

Hoodooed by the delights of daylight saving,
The ear hears something sonorous in summer
Time. With the naiveté of a seasonal newcomer,
Not yet wise to the ways of the late light behaving
So brightly, & overloaded branches waving
Overhead, the senses become numb, the dumber
Habitués of such overheated hinterlands'
Lax luxuriance so unlike the dry-point engraving
Under the lush oil painting of midsummer
Which overlays spare, sketchy winter lands.

183

Who disappeared before you saw them last—
In fact you cannot remember when or where—
Apparently vanished into clandestine air,
Into aerial vistas lymphatically overcast,
Unemphatic as their undercover past,
For which nobody has an afterthought to spare.
At the speed of thought or even faster,
The days since this dereliction sped by fast
With the mad acceleration of despair,
An aftermath anticlimactic as disaster.

184

Like my home this poem, well furnished yet unfinished—
Its informal lay-out fundamentally unchanged,
Though some stanzaic rooms remain to be rearranged—
Remains in its over-all dimensions somehow diminished.
Imagination dormant, skill undiminished,
Long winded afflatus abnormally short-changed,
Infinitely capable & worthy of expansion,
This work, while incomplete, must still be finished,
The grace restored that never was estranged,
A workhouse made up in a dilapidated mansion.

185

For years & years & day by day I kept
Faith with this candid, understanding page
On which, as if on an illuminated stage,
I eviscerated myself, rejoiced, & wept
In ennui. Today my diary overslept,
While I was up early, anxious to disengage
From sleep, impatient for dawn as if waiting for a friend.
Yet here, scribbled in a script cryptic & inept,
Lay the records of a middling middle age
Between brilliant beginnings & an indeterminate end.

186

On paging through last year bound in red leather
Whose returning leaves refurbished an overlook
But no advance, I murmured "Go on, silly book,
Lighter than lead yet heavier than a feather,
Diurnal record of the dirty weather whether
The heavens grumbled or the groundwork shook.
No autobiography wants a hero.
Multiplying minus & minus together
Produces a plus, a principle I mistook
For the sad fact that zero times zero equals zero."

187

Appalled at the return of yesterday,
Though chronically uncertain of the date,
If extraordinarily constrained to wait,
Patients become ornery, impatient of delay.
Disgusted by the detritus of today,
Tomorrow presents an empty wall, a vacant slate,
Apart from a few forgettable appointments.
So much undone & nothing left to say,
The faith one aimed to break will be betrayed too late
To avoid all daily disappointments.

188

So there you are & here I am. How treasure
Your presence, since my presents were a bribe
To coax from the bosom of an alien tribe,
With patents of security & leisure,
An agent whose impatience patience cannot measure?
What catastrophe, too predictable to describe,
Brought you back at last, awkward, always on your guard in
Transparent armour, impervious to pleasure,
Almost, neither quite a lover nor a scribe,
& yet content to be lost & found in this garden?

189

That happiness that has so much to teach,
From fantastical fact to scienterrific fiction,
Risks someday becoming an addiction.
This blameless day that nothing can impeach,
Beyond reproach yet never out of reach,
If only in the picturesque depiction
Of our dilapidated pleasure dome,
With such facetious but unfunny turns of speech
As grammatical slapstick & addlepated diction,
Suggests a felicity that will nevermore leave home.

190

Fast friendships, quick acquaintances, both brittle
& translucent as this fragile china cup,
May be broken as any home can be busted up.
Affiliates too petty to belittle,
Lickspittle belittlers, will in a little
Be discarded or forgiven or shut up
In the breakfront cupboard of recollection.
Bits cracked or smashed, if dusted off & fixed up
With difficulty, goodwill, glue or spittle,
Add to one's quasipermanent collection.

191

Look backwards regretfully on our ecstasy.
Our pasts in shambles & our backs uncovered,
Like infatuated hummingbirds we hovered
Above the background of comparative sanity
For what resembled an eternity,
Till, recovering our senses, we discovered
The true sense of ecstasy which means, of course,
"A standing out"—an outstanding possibility
Once guaranteed by certain sugar-covered
Moments eventually subject to remorse.

192

As an aspect of recovery, unpacking
Has-beens, & unhappily glancing back
At each thankless stack, takes me so aback,
Finding forever something or someone lacking,
I trash the past & send the fragments packing
Backwards down their retroactive track.
For what am I to do with all that sad-sack stuff
Which I make such a bad practice of ransacking
For an answer I shall be glad to lack:
Was enough too much, or is too much not enough?

193

Though the long-distance runner seemed like a slow-starter,
Often as not reluctant to get out of bed
As a convalescent or a newlywed,
As he sped through speculative realms art can hardly charter,
Which might render an old tartar understandably tarter
At the expense of the overpaid & underbred
Competition, your unique voice
As much as your own pace made you a martyr
To the commonplace, already & forever unread,
But at the finish line there may be reason to rejoice.

194

It is almost quiet enough to hear yourself thinking—
As if one could ever really hear oneself think
Or listen to the turgid stream of consciousness sink
Into silence, its tributaries shrinking
Drop by drop into a stagnant, stinking
Styx as deep as death & black as ink,
Where not even fantasy is problem-free.
Which miracle would be worthwhile rethinking
As you transubstantiate your daily drink
From the water of thought into the wine of poetry.

195

Forged in the heart of the fire, fired in the forge of the heart,
This vessel, not of iron or clay but of molten flesh,
Will emerge unglazed, intemperate, fragile & fresh
As today from the oven of which it was parcel & part,
As a fiction, a fusion of nature & art,
Almost flawless yet always to be fashioned afresh
In necessity over & over & over again,
Never finished, ever refinished anew from the start,
Till the maker & his material mesh,
Incandescent, reformed & refined into an ominous Amen.

196

One of these days will be one of those
Days when stuff happens not as it has done;
Anon some heteronymous anyone
Wonders when the calendar will disclose
Days like this, free verse as opposed to prose
Days on which no one hopes to see the sun.
This unhoped-for envelope encloses
A proposal: only those indisposed may suppose
Days multifarious & not half so much fun
As the sleight of hand with which a poem closes.

197

Where will the kill-joy principle of order,
As It Were's simple-minded sibling *As Is*,
Revisit the subjective provinces of his
Former stand-offs, in order to supplant disorder
Along a long-disputed, undefended border,
All pleasant vistas & shady businesses,
Odious wasteland or melodious woodland,
Rural splendour or suburban sordor,
Or the extraordinarily ordinary, *viz.*
The spot where notoriously spotty Justice would land?

198

Given those sole alternatives, fight or flight,
You cannot fight who cannot stand, although
No feckless fugitive knows anywhere to go.
In the face of frightful adversity you might
Be surprised at the warlike appetite
& courage desperation may bestow.
Wanting deadly weapons, a word instead of a stone,
Unable to decide between right & right,
Each distinct as day & night & yes & no,
Try the flight from the alone to the Alone.

199

Pain, in the nature of experience,
Remained today the same as every day,
Much as I wished that it would go away,
Make or take or fake its departure hence,
Seeing that its presence made no sense
Since ultimately it had nothing left to say.
Denied, deplored, but yet besought & beckoned,
Death will look like the last & least of accidents.
Who would ask such an unwelcome guest to stay
When its persistence must be reckoned by the second?

200

Because you do not travel time stands still
Or would seem to, were it not for an expense
Of space. You cannot view its monuments
Unless you stand upon a little hill—
And by *unless* of course I mean *until*—
Along a long vista of impermanent events,
To glimpse a façade through falling foliage.
Despite the false allurements of *was* and *will*,
Try to continue in the omnipresent tense,
In view of that penultimate folly, age.

201

Nightfall falls, decisive as a knife,
Across the glassy smooth, translucent lawn
Which all sorts of shadowy shapes have splashed upon,
As across a bland & checkered, cluttered life,
Incomplete with cashiered checks & smothered strife,
Until up comes the blank, inevitable dawn
As abrupt as some giant gleaming guillotine.
So daylight will precede an afterlife
That, as far as no one knows will go on & on,
Till the curtain descends on this immemorable scene.

202

Enrolled in the summer school of sensual knowledge
An ignoramus seduces himself self-taught,
Slyly exploiting all the misinformation he got
From erotic revery & innocuous self-knowledge,
The gnostic body he long has longed to acknowledge
As misbegotten & as autonomically fraught
As the preposterous laws of perpetual motion.
Drop-outs from this semiotic seasonal college
May pick up what its graduates forgot
Against the background of the plunging, lunging ocean.

203

This is not a picture of my house,
Nor a simulacrum. You are here,
Or anyway you know I wish you were
If only so that I might introduce
You to this space as special as a spouse
To me, wherein familiar appear
All the cherished furniture of home.
Of little resale value but some use
As reminders remaindered, less a sinecure
Than a temporary pleasure dome.

204

A window opens in the Western wall
Of my disorderly, reordered study
Where I translate & write but do not study
Studies never studied there at all—
Lucus a non lucendo. I watch the fall
Of foliage that has turned fuddy-duddy
In a slow & silent picture show,
While wondering why anyone would want to call
This golden, deliquescent, ruddy, bloody
Grove a grove because it does not glow.

205

Reverberating like a terminus
With the destinations of departed trains,
The overstimulated brain retains
Numerous variegated, verminous
Notions more or less coterminous
With plaintive prospects & emotive plains,
As if faith & doubt could coexist,
Which, while abortive, come to term in us,
Lines no schedule or rhyme scheme explains,
The metaphorical trains of thought one missed.

206

Cherish, so long as there is time to cherish
The present tense until it shall have passed
Into the unconditionally past
Perfection of a semitransparent, squarish
Ice cube, whose usefulness must perish
With the form its fluid substance must outlast,
Like a moment eternally surpassing
Itself in a blink of day's wide open, garish
Eye when instantaneously overcast:
A panorama continually passing.

207

Ornery, the laws of effect & cause,
If inexorable, sometime seem perverse,
As when a casual excuse is worse,
If implausible, than your real reason was.
But that chance concatenation cannot pause
For long & never functions in reverse—
A palindrome our laws will not allow.
Often afterwards but not always because
Follows everywhere in the logical universe;
Yet what was then determines what is now.

208

On retracing the errors of the botanical
Maze where nature is no metaphor—
For what in heaven's name could it stand for?—
Your enthusiasm seemed mechanical
As the dreams of a saturnine, Satanical
Moping, minatory minotaur,
Adumbrating the rude apology you wrote.
Tomorrow sorrow's maniacal manacle,
The iron jewelry you wore,
Will find no antidote in an anecdote.

209

There are certain things which one would rather have done
Than have to do, & not a few that you would be glad to
        have not,
Not only in foolish foresight but in futile afterthought,
Marathons anybody else might have liked to have run
You would hate to run; laurels effortlessly won
Will be forgotten, unlike the failures one never forgot.
The perfect future remains unfinished because
No future perfect undertakings will have been begun.
What one ought not to have done eclipses all that one ought;
Regret is merely envy of a self that never was.

210

Omens may be anything almost,
An umbrella open inside the house, the flight
Of birds, whether from the left or on the right,
Spilled salt, a broken mirror, all or most
Mute & incomprehensible as a ghost
Or the zodiac enlightening the night
With some pseudo-scientific explanation.
A soul by arbitrary signs engrossed
Might miss the whole point: no omen might
Mean a thing except in interpretation.

211

To this last, reanimated room
What sad enthusiasm drags me back,
Or somatic terrorist attack,
Attracted to the atavistic gloom
That is a characteristic of the tomb
Or womb, after an absence like a lack
Of assonance? Here in confidence I kept
That phantom personality of whom
The sun & moon & altered stars kept track
As I anachronistically slept.

212

There are no surprises in the past
Whose shadowy, old-fashioned furniture,
As uncomfortable as it is obscure,
Ugly however lovingly amassed,
Was after all not ever made to last;
But we are nothing if not what we were,
An abstract canvas or a window curtain
Across an aperture that gives, aghast,
Upon a view, imperfect, to be sure,
Provisional, precarious, & far from certain.

213

As the everyday miasma lifts
Or breaks up a bit around the edges,
Loss, with its protocols & privileges—
For even desolation brings some gifts—
Discounts its hidden poverty & sifts
Through leftovers & the bets it hedges
For excuses not to feel so sad.
Imperceptibly as depression drifts
Away, experience confirms what hope alleges:
Perhaps tomorrow will not be too bad?

214

Spirit might be defined as a deficit:
Silver tarnishes & cotton wrinkles;
Similes simplify, a symbol tinkles;
All such deficiencies will benefit
The genuine articles which they befit
As definitely as glass cracks & paper crinkles,
Things redefined by negative definition,
When the indefinite becomes the definite.
Do we call the Spring a spring because it sprinkles,
Incidentally coincidental with its repetition?

215

How often one wishes all of it were true,
Not infrequently relieved that it is not,
Whenever reminded of everything one ought
Or ought not to have done or ought to do!
How many were chosen arbitrarily, while so few
Were called! Assuming it is all a plot
Experienced but never understood,
You cannot see anything which you see through.
Truth is opaque. What does it matter what
Is true or good as gold, compared to wood?

216

Perspective, of the eye or of the mind,
A perception or a metaphor
For peaking through a window or a door,
That perfection it took centuries to find
In the West but which eluded the refined
Pictographers of the yellow emperor,
Realigns the sight-lines of previous existence:
Events we have negligently left behind,
Unlike the obstacles that loom before,
Offer uncertain optical resistance.

217

This oblique glacier, like a postage stamp
Stuck upon the slaggy mountainside,
Provides a band-aid hardly adequate to hide
The stony staircase or the rocky ramp
Up cliff-faces dangerous when damp,
To which ragged tatters of old ice are tied.
Oppressed by grit & grime & gravity,
Still it glistens, a superannuated vamp,
As millennia of snowfalls slide
Off top-lofty summits into an ample cavity.

218

Unlike the underworld of television,
The interactive wonderland of books,
Whether cheap paperbacks or in *de luxe*
Editions, invites immediate revision,
Backward glances, instead of a straightforward vision,
Seldom as interesting as it looks,
Predicated on the primacy of time.
Whereas afterthought & indecision,
The obvious clue one always overlooks,
Plot what one can pick up or put down anytime.

219

No doubt I thought too much about the past
Before, which after all cannot return,
Although I once had memories to burn,
Like the devastated pages of that vast
Diary which I reread aghast,
Too many & embarrassing to turn.
As it starts to look like this time was the last time,
The beginning & the middle go by fast
Enough, till it is easy to discern
The end. Time passed is no more than a pastime.

220

As if stepping from one room into the next,
Not always remembering to close the door
Between behind one altogether, or
Leaving it ajar on some pretext,
One wakes inexpressibly perplexed
By memories too muddled to ignore,
A world of indeterminate extremes,
& territories oneirically annexed.
What conscientious recollection can restore,
Once vanished, the never-never-land of dreams?

221

This stream, however frivolous & fickle,
Flows one way & cannot be reversed,
As if forever putting first things first.
Its superfluity distills a trickle
Down to make a muckle of a mickle,
Which if wasted is not readily reimbursed.
The inevitable becomes abhorrent
As that spectre represented with a sickle,
Of all specious bogeymen the worst,
When the trickle turns into a torrent.

222

Although historically your geocentric
Orthodoxy depended on your point of view
& a short-sighted natural world-view,
Limited & unabashedly egocentric,
We now know reality as heliocentric,
Proving appearances to be untrue.
Counterintuitive, perhaps perverse,
Our everyday orbit, nonetheless eccentric,
Describes my revolution about you.
There is no centre to the universe...

223

Unless yourself, that focus of resentment
Less exceptional than generous appears,
For all the rivalries of the evolving years.
Of every slight, what every event meant,
Envy pathetically faked present presentment,
Till taunts attenuated with no tears
Made a visitation of each visit.
Incivility & its discontentment
Left our love in permanent arrears.
But this is not the end of everything, is it?

224

Nothing more conventional than dress
Appears, unless the vagaries of spelling.
However customized, what common dwelling
Features as anything than an address,
Seldom more but ordinarily less,
A tautology that seems hardly worth retelling?
Not to mention that ultimate convention we call style.
& yet originality, nonetheless,
At once disconcerting & compelling,
Surprises like a sudden, gratuitous smile.

225

Cold fingers those depleted trees which will
In autumn's paradox appear to smoulder
Flamboyantly. Tomorrow will feel colder
Still than today & yesterday, until
The overheated world begins to chill
As the advances of the frost grow bolder.
Among the advantages of growing old,
Beside the pleasures of rereading, is the thrill,
Nostalgic, intensified as one grows older,
That accompanies intimations of the cold.

226

December commences & the frost relents.
Yet a few survivors hang on after all.
The inconsistencies of winter, summer, spring & fall
Suggest a certain lack of confidence.
Today is as mild as yesterday was intense,
As if the calendar were always on recall.
Leaves clog the eaves & carpet the veranda
&, uncollected, wither into decadence.
Winter reexamines what will soon befall:
The proliferation of Autumn's propaganda.

227

Leaves fall & our neighbours reappear,
Concealed all summer by a screen of leaves.
Autumn sees what summer disbelieves
In, as these hitherto invisible aliens draw near.
So in a rear-view mirror images appear
More proximate than anyone believes.
Anyway those next door are our neighbours
Normally no more than half a year;
The proximity which foliage bereaves
Us of the ostentatious Fall belabours.

228

Like the brief achievement of cold fusion,
As battalions of kamikaze snowflakes squall
Where leaves fell yesterday (a few still fall)
& proliferate in prodigal profusion,
Our thought experiment proved an illusion
Whose silliness seemed mythological;
This heresy adheres like one last leaf
Which stark branches cling to in confusion
But will ultimately shudder to recall
Once relinquished in chill disbelief.

229

Who has, if no two snowflakes are the same,
The curiosity to count them all,
Watching them fall, wayward as they fall,
Idiosyncratic, each without a name
Like an evanescent, frozen flame,
Individual & not identical?
Innumerable every time it snows,
In their anonymous billions they became
Like stanzas variously metrical,
Or free verse marginally worse than prose.

230

To live through all four seasons & survive
What seemed a good idea at the time,
From chaste winter to seductive summertime,
&, without appearing to repine, to strive
To do no more than merely stay alive
& walk upright although you cannot climb,
Qualifies as the secret of survival.
Yet seasons leave as soon as they arrive
Or sooner, like punishment preceding crime,
As often departure anticipates arrival.

231

The summer solstice once marked the start of summer
In the vicinity of June the twenty-first,
When the high tide of daylight was reversed.
Formerly formally celebrated as midsummer,
This prematurely middle-aged newcomer
Epitomizing of all days the longest but not the worst,
Presents an eternal present, enemy of the past,
In view of a future ever duller & dumber
Than the number of days remaining to be rehearsed,
Each one a smidgin shorter than the last.

232

The whole world is our waiting room, & I'm
On time for my appointment, more or less.
Too late for love, too early for success,
Still I continue working overtime,
Believing unpunctuality a crime.
We cannot know, although we try to guess
The hour of our ultimate appointment
For which no one can help but be on time.
The diagnosis? Less distress
Than disillusionment & disappointment.

233

Weary of being an incarnate being—
As if there were another way to live
Or some viable alternative
To feeling, tasting, smelling, hearing, seeing
(Not to mention sweating, shitting, peeing!),
I cannot help but wonder how I can forgive
The flesh for its indignities & pain.
The disgusted spirit that requires freeing
Has nothing but indifference to give
Till death will come as welcome as the rain.

234

After each nocturnal episode
A day extends immaculate as snow
Which, however overcast, will glow
Like a grove that never truly glowed.
Anyone who overnight bestrode
A nightmare, nonetheless aspires to go
Hopefully to heaven or nirvana.
What all those poems I once wrote in code
Meant, I only know I do not know,
Except they came gratuitous as manna.

235

The next page of your diary remains
Forever immaculately blank
Until invested like a savings bank
With afterthoughts & inscrutable ink stains,
Outmoded clichés & meaningless refrains,
The remainders of an extinct style that stank,
All leftovers of a less than golden age.
If yesterday it snowed while today it rains,
Today has only yesterday to thank
For this watermarked & tear-stained page.

236

Like water inadvertently misspent,
Time once wasted cannot be restored,
Unlike such funds as one may hope to hoard
Or invest at an exorbitant per cent.
Waste is that of which one must repent,
Though often in a way its own reward.
Rivulet or cataract, ice-
Bound in its precipitous descent,
Or meandering through the landscape, as if bored:
Who says one cannot step into it twice?

237

The sun is a long-distance runner: wait for it,
As if you awaited the beginning of a minute waltz.
As I've said before, all metaphors are false,
However approximately they may fit.
Attend the splendiferous rays of mother wit,
As well as wisdom's elemental salts,
Were time not a marathon runner but a sprinter
More ancient than the sun, could it remit
The penalties attentive on the faults
That punctuate the illustrious sports of winter?

238

My mother was a glacier; suckled at that frozen teat,
I learned to love not hot or tepid but frosty water.
Breast-fed by the northland's haughty eldest daughter,
I thrived on a liquid diet of vodka, gin, & aquavit,
Till, fledged on the wings of the North Wing wild & fleet,
I swam as a swan & dived as a sea otter,
All before I was no more than five years old,
When at last I was baptized in Love's firewater,
Swift was my soul to answer him & jubilant my feet,
Whose heart is ardent though his extremities are cold.

239

Given a material world of wood & plastic,
Your paradigm shifts. But what is a paradigm,
Unless a categorical waste of time,
Diagrammatic, grammatical &/or onomastic?
Imagination, never iconoclastic
To a fault, holds up nomenclature as sublime,
While the nameless universe, forever on display,
Adrastic as nemesis & fatally fantastic,
Sometimes fails & sometimes almost seems to rhyme,
Till the stream falls silent that had so much to say.

240

People who don't talk do make me nervous,
As if affronted by the still equivocation of the grave
Where there is nothing left to say or save.
Yet what is there in silence to unnerve us
When in the intervals of some divine communion service
One finds oneself virtually speechless as a slave?
Speech craves speech. The languid & loquacious,
God knows how they reciprocally deserve us,
Unlike the superlatively beautiful & brave
Whose watchword is mum as their mumchance is
        ungracious.

241

Procrastinate, it's later than you think,
& you've thought long enough for one short day,
Or wrong enough. Mistakes must take a holiday,
But no vacation will stay you from the brink
Of extinction, waiting for another sun to sink
Into a darkness no forethought may delay,
To be erased except in afterthought.
The distinctness of yesterday begins to shrink
Till the best of it is that it was yesterday,
Or if not the best, anyway all we've got.

242

One watchword, work now, worry later.
While never too late to procrastinate,
Why try to anticipate the very fate
You wait for, dilatory as a waiter
Or an overcrowded elevator
Freighted with the melancholy weight
Of memory, oblivion's step-daughter?
What impatient prestidigitator
Can persuade a wavering wave to wait
On what was simultaneous as water?

243

"On love, on grief on every human thing,"
The epigrammatist Walter Savage Landor
Remarked with his habitual savvy candor,
"Time sprinkles Lethe's water with his wing."
Time so personified could be anything
With wings: a hummingbird, a crow, a goose or gander,
A pterodactyl. As for Lethe's water,
Having been dipped in that revivifying spring—
Deeper than hell & colder, more forgiving, grander—
I think oblivion to be memory's daughter.

244

You will forget nothing in the syllabic long & short
Run, conserved by illiberal emotion:
The mind resembles some overwhelming pacific ocean,
Yet is simultaneously sharp as a tax report
& indomitable as a boy's cardboard toy fort,
Emollient & slick as balsamic lotion.
Who, walking without a walker, can talk without
A talker to talk to? What will conceives will seldom self-abort.
The divine being such a curious notion,
While belief remains disbelief, what is there left to doubt?

245

Your poem is not a happening unless
Qualified to earn its living on easy street.
Innocuous, unpolished yet incomplete,
A lyric may do nothing save confess
Its shortcomings, its method a metrical hit & mess,
Not a treatise nor a treatment but a treat.
Fluctuating like the waves of the sea, my rhyme,
Indifferent to failure & success,
Goes forth on tiny catalectic feet,
Primed to solve yet never to commit a crime.

246

Never wait, for waiting is a waste
Of time. I seldom waited for a second,
& never, ever whenever the muses beckoned,
Especially when beguiled below the waist.
If iceberg lettuce & hothouse tomatoes taste
The same, i.e. tepid, their shelf-life is reckoned
Along with the ripeness of all mortal produce
Which time, which is notoriously two-faced,
Distasteful & tasteless, chaste yet oh! so fecund,
When properly spaced out will still produce.

247

You are of yourself the pattern of
Perfection, as *la famille verte* & *famille rose* disdain
Other varieties of porcelain.
Perfections which maintain the character of love,
Below the beltway as in heaven above,
Demonstrate how much success embodied pain,
A lachrymose & saccharine confection
Like the fall of the sparrow & the wings of the dove:
Anyway, it was always too late to complain,
Since in truth we all partake of imperfection.

248

Temporary, muddled & abject,
A mud-puddle reflects the cloudy sky
Which finds itself sublimely mirrored by
Any still pond or highly polished object.
But you are ever a transcendental subject,
Reflecting conversely me, myself & I,
As it contains & overflows
The same flawed & changeable love-object
Which inhabits neither a palace nor a sty,
With all the imperfections it may enclose.

249

To the doors of paradise forgiveness provides a hinge.
Who claims that he has nothing to forgive
Renounces revenge as an alternative,
Unlike the vindictive who cringe & wail & whinge,
& so the silver swan behind her reedy fringe
Of rushes would rather die than live & let live.
Forgiven not seven times but seventy times seven,
One day the abstemious will booze & binge
Until there will be nothing left to give
Away beside all the choir & furniture of heaven.

250

Playing with fire, like skating on thin ice,
Were equally insouciant & dangerous
In one sense, not to be too censorious,
No more risk-free than solitary vice.
So I hesitated to follow the well-meant advice
I thought meretricious if meritorious.
The Fall of Man struck me as perpendicular,
Predicated on a mere throw of the dice,
While Love, immodest, mute, vainglorious,
Taught me the world, that gaming-hell, was circular.

251

As I sit here smoking up the storm,
As our ancestral shamans used to do,
& as with every puff I think of you
Who are of all superlatives the norm,
As unexpected as a thunderstorm,
As transient & refreshing as the dew,
With few to love & next to none to praise,
My feelings roil & my ideas swarm,
Fantastical but often all too true.
My American Spirit moves me in sundry ways.

252

American Spirits, Camels, Lucky Strikes—
Each was at one time or other a favourite brand,
Not to mention those I used to roll by hand.
Theoretically it is the nicotine one likes,
Productive of such brief euphoric spikes
As no total abstainer can understand,
Who deprecates the dangers of cigarettes,
Especially in the grubby hands of tykes.
While many imagine that they cannot stand
The second-hand aroma, it is the taste no one forgets.

253

I smoke my cigarettes in segments as
I waste my life, one installment at a time,
As if smoking had become a reprehensible crime,
As in fact it practically has,
Along with drinking & kinky sex & all that jazz,
Not to mention the obsolete intervals of rhyme.
Yet a day seldom passes without invoking
The god of tobacco & his dazzling razzmatazz
With its verbal paraphernalia. Apparently I'm
Addicted to this serial poem as to serial smoking.

254

Belief begs many questions of the moon;
Disbelief disappoints you with an answer
From some anachronistic necromancer
Who can interpret any anagram or rune
As a balloon in an apolitical cartoon
Yet cannot contemplate a cure for cancer.
Shall we subject the moonlight to analysis?
This gritty pearl is like a titty prune.
& who can resist the advances of that astral dancer
With all her mountains, plains & seas & pleasure palaces.

255

Lies before sunrise: whoever skated on
& over the slippery ice rink of the night,
Finally fed up with fighting an almost hopeless fight
Before the specious enlightenment of dawn,
Insomniac, will place all his expectancies upon
Some last Imam, hidden in plain sight
Of human love, all sleeplessness surpassing.
Then the simple, necessary light outshone
The abyss, so brave, innocuous & bright:
7:35. Time's business is passing.

256

Of magical mystifications there are as many
As crippling diseases: mutual love
&, after dry spells, the replenishment thereof,
&, though many pretend there aren't any,
Natural mysteries turn up like a bad penny,
Enveloping creation like a glove.
A mystery, which may be anything,
Such as the sky that fell on Henny-Penny,
The earth beneath us & the heavens above,
Unveils the clarification of evening.

257

As the anxiety of evening
Resolves our evolutionary love,
When tongues of flame & the descending dove
Through opposition find an opening
For happiness that constitutes a happening
Past prejudice & pride & prurient self-love,
We two, too few, become the mysterious many
Whom reduplicated love's reopening
Is itself the evidence & emblem of—
Self-evident, that is, if there be any!

258

There is one game only. Circumstance
Can vary, but variety remains
Constant. What one unlucky punter gains
Another loses in the rigged game of chance.
Similarly with what passes for romance,
Whose alternating ecstasies & pains
Add up to nothing more permanent than a game,
Despite such introductions to the dance,
What another lost is all that one regains,
The rules of the game eternally the same.

259

At dawn I rose to don my singing-robe,
At dawn, when the Eastern sky was robed with rose,
&, clothed in imaginary majesty, arose
To put on my old, tattered tartan robe.
As the trees outside my window were seen to disrobe
& the overgrown evergreen vista froze,
I composed a palinode to the Necessary,
Too shy to pry, too curious not to probe,
Superimposing praise upon quotidian prose,
The imaginative upon the imaginary.

260

This world, to the extent that it is real,
Material, unsophisticated, rude,
& imprudent, is not unlikely to intrude,
Like some Rudesby in the middle of a meal,
Or the truth before the conclusion of a deal,
Into your sylvan or suburban solitude.
Whatever it is, it is not delusive:
The world as will is never far from ideal,
However rambunctious, contradictory, crude,
As transubstantial as it is elusive.

261

Lore & order: to give what it takes.
On the other hand, it takes what it gives.
Illegal lore historically forgives
Our infantile, infinitesimal mistakes
That figure in the figurative out-takes
In which increasingly one lives.
Forgiven, the irritability & teasing,
Outlived, the unanswered interrogatives
& ennui endured for both our sakes,
When order consoled & law was not displeasing!

262

The end of an era, unlike the end of the street,
Cannot be recorded in a photograph.
Lies that showed up on no polygraph
Adumbrate life-histories replete,
From swaddling bands to winding sheet,
With music—could one but fix the phonograph!
The end of the day should be no more than a metaphor
For a work which, while still imperfect & incomplete,
Registers positively off the graph.
The reef impends, yet we are not far from the shore.

263

The water that sloshes over the top of a rock
Will not wash it away until the backwash brings
Back the echoes which the ocean rings
With, its bubbling babble & black backtalk.
The whole earth ticks like an atomic clock,
Erotically, as to itself it sings
Long rhapsodies atonal & amatory.
An argosy, a bottomless laughing-stock,
The sea produces many peculiar things
Some of which are pertinent to our story.

264

If the world were your oyster what would be the shell?
Unquestionably, a pair of glasses
(Such as were thought to distinguished the chattering classes
Who could speculatively speculate & spell),
Plastic, nor gold nor horn nor tortoiseshell
Frames, whose workmanship their material surpasses,
Surround the naked eye's unvariegated
Spectacles. How can you ask or tell
At whom the suspect object may make passes?
O! for a distant view unmediated!

265

Things that have gone missing & do not fit
Will be less easily realized than idealized
Before their absence can be analyzed.
As you sense your sudden descent into the pit
& feel your self reprogrammed into an *it*,
As if your very being had been vandalized
Then reconstituted or restored in error.
Being nontransferable, not every bit
Of your existence can be personalized.
& yet of your being lost I live in terror.

266

Though earth may serve unworthy as your urn
The universe will prove your cenotaph;
The praise that may be aired on your behalf
Takes no account of what you failed to earn.
With all the alien funeral pyres that burn
Like distant dots on a celestial graph,
You will not go unnoticed when you go,
Nor as a ghost eternally return
Unheard, like those low notes below the staff,
As silent & invisible as snow.

267

Where have the silent constellations gone?
Above our heads the friendless skies are blank,
For which we have our own urbanity to thank,
Before a premonition of the dawn
The heavens' storied enchiridion,
With their imaginary portents, sank
Below the horizon, only to rise again
As stories vaster than the space they were drawn upon,
Stored in some half-forgotten memory bank,
Hieratic, fascinating, plain.

268

Nothing frightening in the depths but height,
In colourful heaven or monochromatic hell,
Revealing light & concealing dark as well.
But there is much to be afraid of in the light
Of day, whose specious & nefarious delight
Even the clear-sighted cannot tell
From darkness. The ill-illuminated dread the dark,
So comfortless, obnoxious & impolite,
The realm in which departed spirits dwell,
The shore for which in time we all embark.

269

Opting out of an enchanted pentagram,
I find the world as I left it, half-baked & square
As some deservedly obscure & shabby city square
Incongruously pandemoniac as a traffic jam,
& see, not as I was but as I am,
Myself in ruins almost beyond repair.
I pray the gratuitous afflatus will recur again
& that my magical self-possession turn out not to be a sham,
Gathering as only answer to my prayer
The disillusionment that disguises pain.

270

Empty as the inside of a vase
When the flower arrangement has fallen apart,
Or as an abandoned grocery cart,
Meaningless as a disqualifying clause
Or an audience's perfunctory applause
At the pointless pyrotechnics of performing art,
Nothing seems so vacant as an unoccupied dress,
Unless than in interstellar space there never was
Any vacuum so total as a devastated heart,
The human epitome of emptiness.

271

The gulf between creators & consumers,
Seems obvious, traversable though great:
We all consume, but do not all create,
Whether prodigies or too late bloomers,
New tunes, new rules, new recipes & rumours,
Serial music & the dystopic welfare state.
Never condescend to the consumptive past
With its imperative moods & humourless humours;
With any luck this morning will recreate
Consumer goods too good not to last.

272

Like a cotton-polyester blend
That turns out to be pure polyester,
Like lilies that notoriously fester
Faster than fresh weeds, too foul to comprehend,
Casual associations end
In a period or half-semester.
Yet friendship is not friendship which can alter
The unofficial office of a friend
Who comes to comfort & remains to pester:
Sincere & abrasive, friendship will not falter.

273

It seems as if there has always been two teams.
In Byzantium these were called the greens & the blues,
Between which there was nothings much to choose.
The green of contemplation versus the deep blue of dreams,
Provided this morning one of my favourite themes.
Opposites collide & beautiful bruisers bruise,
As if mankind were fundamentally divided
Against itself in an end-game that seems
All too antagonistic to amuse,
Hemispheres perennially two-sided.

274

To save a pittance unprofitably gained
Compared to that which life & time & fortune loses,
Morbid, sordid parsimony refuses
To recognize the regime discomfort complained
Of, the losses our economy sustained,
With all the remains of property one uses
Till used up gaily on a daily basis.
Yet what was lost will never be regained,
Since poverty is not the mother of the Muses,
Nor yet of the uncomfortable Graces.

275

Awake at 3 A.M., after I took
A soporific at 12:40,
Out of tune as a pianoforte,
I neither shuddered in aftershock nor shook
With excitement. How could one be mistook
For precocious when so far over 40?
At 74, my sordid mortality scorning
Like an abandoned, half-read dirty book,
Bed-ridden, I am still incurably sporty,
Soon to be reborn into phantasmagorical morning.

276

The mood music that usually flowed through me
Silently suddenly has ceased to surge,
The source from which those tunes used to emerge,
Curtailed, cut off & utterly shut up to me,
Aborting the resources of the true me.
Absent any unutterable urge.
I miss that inspirational insurgency,
The furious muses that choose not to pursue me,
Willy-nilly, to the verge
Of further metrical emergency.

277

Plainly to have taken a vow of poverty
& repudiated all ostentatious wealth,
Giving up everything, including good looks & health,
You live, my love, in total penury,
But for the prospect of incipient greenery
Announcing spring's revolutionary commonwealth.
As you are so poor perhaps I am too rich
In material things, & one day may pay the penalty
When love steals away my worldly goods by stealth,
Substituting who was who for which is which.

278

Another day! Another frigging stanza!
Periodically I wonder what is wrong
With the false quantities of this awkward song,
Yet every morning comes as a bonanza
Sometimes in the form of some phantom *esperanza,*
& though the many may fault my work as all too long,
Just because I did not choose to tell a story,
Look at Don Quixote and Sancho Panza,
Whose suit was futile & whose suit was strong.
Then condemn all art as masturbatory!

279

Though every day seems slightly different,
Every night appears by & large the same;
Days may be wild; nights nowadays are tame,
Predetermined & as yet impenitent,
&, in retrospect, perhaps, perfectly indifferent.
Each day may be reconsidered as a game.
Distant, impressionistic & impaired,
The recollection of time so misspent
Would be a waste of spirit, except when it became
The precious present of time shared.

280

Such ambiguous symptoms as disturb
Me, the stoop, the shuffle & the shakes,
Unavoidable missteps, the small mistakes
Which conscientious care can neither cure nor curb,
Were nothing compared to the errors that perturb
This maker of unconscionable fakes,
Whose tuneful exuberance proliferates, to be pruned
Of over-reliance on adverbs & the copula verb.
Psychosomatic pain is all it takes
To convince us every poem is an open wound.

281

So long & longingly anticipated,
That love that lingered on the precipice
Has settled in at last, snatched out of the abyss
Of a bliss which I believed unreciprocated
But turns out to have been reciprocated
All along. With the exception of a kiss,
Mutual confession obviates confusion.
Such satisfaction is not soon satiated.
Reciprocal & egalitarian, this
Love, no more than class, is an illusion.

282

Lying in, the world whirls on without
You, as mainly it does anyway when you're awake,
& all its blatant advertisements fail to take
You in. There nothing dubious about
You that would lead the underworld to doubt
You, & the undertakings you undertake.
Although such laziness is not a sin,
Waking with a murmur or a shout,
You may think you committed a mistake
In the laid-back luxury of lying in.

283

What if everything were to tumble down
Like a pack of cards, to counterfeit a cliché,
& what if it all were suddenly swept away
By a flood impetuous enough to drown
Me as I sit here in my dressing-gown,
Lazily confounding work & play,
In a catastrophe unpredictable & all but lawless,
Inverting your smile upside down into a frown?
While I have loved you although you were not gay,
I never loved you because I thought you flawless.

284

This image, water flowing over stone,
Came unbidden on the brink of sleep.
Smooth was the stone; the water, clear but deep,
Washed over me as I lay still sleepless, prone
Above the chasm of myself alone,
Knowing as I do that stone can weep
Tears that will not improbably be kept
Like dead voices on a gramophone,
Like the arbitrary images that used to seep
Into my watery, rocky soul before I slept.

285

An appetite for water & for sleep
Characterizes my decrepitude,
Along with a tolerance for solitude
Except for the nightly company I keep,
Never less solitary than when asleep.
While nowadays fewer provocatively nude
Blythe bodies bathe in an obscure effulgence.
My thirst for the conscientious, intricate & deep
Love for which I have an aptitude
Can only be satisfied by mutual indulgence.

286

From pain to complaint, from complaint to resignation
Lurches our domestic partnership,
Like some top-heavy, argumentative treasure ship
Named, say, *The Endeavour*. while I, who make creation
Laboriously my daily recreation,
On the look out for the shores of Serendip,
Strip away the veils from the absurd
Sensations of a renascent incarnation
With rhetoric insufficient to reequip
Reality, an ugly thing, & an uglier word.

287

Little remains of your beauty but a smile
(Unlike certain supercilious, smug smirks),
A fading feline phenomenon, that lurks
On your lips like wormwood for a while,
But unpremeditated & without guile,
One of nature's light-hearted masterworks,
An imperturbable resource alight with laughter.
If all that abides in these stanzas is their style,
It does not gush, though it like water works
In the hands of a master, ever defter, dafter.

288

The plagues of age, a plethora of pills
Attend upon my 73rd uncelebrated
Birthday, the arbitrarily dated
Focus of mostly imaginary ills,
& a stroke that will astonish as it kills,
Desire moribund, perversity sedated,
Ill-fated upon an ill-feted precipice,
I gaze down & back on a landscape of mistakes & thrills
Like little lakes & hills, as if every day I waited
For a revelation, maybe of nothing, perchance of bliss.

289

Sidelined at the spectacle of my own life,
Which I observe with declining interest
As simultaneously companion & guest,
Witness of so much foolish striving & useless strife,
How can one believe in any afterlife
Save inanimation & eternal rest
When the sentient sentence comes to a full stop?
Like a smiling bystander with a stylish knife,
You scan the rhyme-scheme, marginally impressed,
Waiting for the final foot to drop.

290

We live in three dimensions, maybe four
Including time, if time is a dimension,
Which I doubt, although I ought to mention
That some metaphysicians maintain there may be more,
Each an introduction or a door
To infinity, an ingenious invention
I repudiate. One world will suffice
Me. What are extra universes for?
Such 'pataphysical pretense exudes pretension.
Let icons be icons, would be my advice.

291

Drowning in consciousness at 4 A.M.
When everything except the air conditioner seemed asleep,
Fighting the unconscious universe, I keep
Awakening to what I am
Becoming. Ignorance & mayhem
Notwithstanding, my wound continues to weep
Amber tears through which I see you
Spontaneous & satiric as an iamb,
Crepuscular as daylight begins to creep
Through the twittering elders of the ICU.

292

We all know who Polyphemus was:
A one-eyed monster in *The Odyssey*, right?
Who sated his insatiable appetite
On human flesh, presumably because
He lived outside the bounds of human laws
Like some kind of pagan anchorite.
Yet "Polyphemus" means "he who talks too much";
That's you, my dear, my independent clause,
My mouthful & my necessary night,
Whom to hear & see is proximate to touch.

293

What if there were no water & no spring
To feed the birds & squirrels with? No matter.
Lost in the foggy field of antimatter
Where a thing no longer is a thing,
I see you as I saw you, beyond my summoning,
April last. *Vale atque ave frater*
My Caesar & centurion, my heir,
You have lots to do, records to shatter,
Who are weaker than water, stronger than any string
Theory, no less ethereal than air.

294

Loving water more than life itself,
That abundance of which too much is not enough,
Immersed in its calmative lymphatic trough,
I drown myself in the element that is myself,
Teetering on a sentimental shelf,
Ready to plunge beyond the reef into the rough
Depths, enriched with ancillary treasure ships
Like the fabulous deep trenches of oneself,
Stuffed with such extraordinary stuff
As liquid pearls at which illicitly one sips.

295

Open the doors a crack & the past will come bustling in,
That past which was never truly past at all,
Or if *passé* in large things perhaps not in small.
Glittering dew drops like a diamond pin
Decorate the shabby afterlife of sin
As a fruit tree overtops a commonplace wall,
Its emerald wings & coral branches hung
With ruby fruit. Where memory silvers tin
The result is this recollected pastoral,
So matter-of-fact, so ingenuous & so young.

296

Picture Age astride his rusty steed,
Grey as a gander, bald as an ostrich egg,
Threatening Death, unshaken if unstable on one leg,
With incremental art & the apostate's creed.
On his electric chair Age makes such speed
As might cause Dis in extremis to renege,
Hades whose satisfied insatiable appetite
Has no earthly parallel for greed,
Whom it were useless to cajole or bribe or beg,
For his yoke is not easy & his quiddity is light.

297

The morning of my unconditional release
Saw a kind of small invisible rain,
Following on the long, hyper-vigilant reign
Of offended convention & the hygiene police.
Disembarking empty-handed after the Golden Fleece,
I took up my ancient paper route again.
Between an endless quest & an impermanent guest
The difference is next to nothing: neither can never cease,
Incessant as that frothy, undulant terrain
That will continue until the sun comes up in the West.

298

Adonis lay in bonds of death upon a stony bed,
Surrounded by little, wicked flickering flames.
Such pictures long outlive their mythic frames,
With his hysterically lamented sacred head,
Painted garish pink & ghastly red,
A representation of the Name of names.
It was never enough to be good & clever,
Any more than it ever will be enough to be dead,
Whether you come in first or last in the Pythian games.
Nox aeterna? No night lasts forever.

299

Nothing to fear! The ghostly visitor
Left no trace whence it had come or wherever gone,
The curtains were closed, the coverlet was on,
The door was locked, no key was in the door,
&, may I add, my soul was oh so sore
With longing since my saviour had long been gone.
The secret night comes pressing on the blind,
Till, lo! they are gone, those visitors of your
Eidetic memory, who linger before the door of healing dawn,
When none such phantoms shall be left behind.

300

& yet, my peach, my pearl, my paragon,
All flesh is hell, & heavenly what is more.
In the footsteps of the last conquistador
Speechless we stand before the naked dawn
With all our beads & shells & feathers on,
Nothing to loathe & everything to adore,
At the influx of civilization, times out of mind,
On the shore of Costa Rica or San Juan,
In Hispaniola or San Salvador,
Gormless, armed & barbarous & blind.

301

& the light that sifted through an open door
Like salt, like sand, as subtle as a smile,
Betrayed no message but a vapid simile, while
The pages that had settled on the floor,
Dusty as lust, undisturbed in wicked semaphore,
Lay like leaves for ages in this elevated peristyle,
To be filed under forget in some elementary alphabet,
As if one had forgotten what it all was intended for:
The silvery foreshore that extends mile after mile
Where the shining sands await us wide & wet.

302

Morning almost dawned pearlescent, perfect,
All but indistinguishable at first from night,
A sight more light than dark, more grey than white,
Handsome & self-righteous as a prefect,
A perfect opening to an imperfect
Day, virginal & like a virgin notoriously tight.
Anxious while the blinds of night are drawn,
Waiting for first light to perfect
Tomorrow's sketchy panoramic oversight,
I lay long awake, longing for the dawn.

303

Save for an illumination in the East,
As the expected day crept into flame,
Nothing changed & everything seemed the same,
Like the stale leftovers of an incredible feast.
Darkness dwindled & the stars decreased,
& what was overnight at once became
The tintype of an obscure camera.
What if I waited till at last you came,
The never forgotten & the undeceased?
O omnia omina in anima!

Notes

1: *Non omnia omina in anima*—"Not all omens (signs or portents) are in the mind or soul". See concluding stanza for affirmative, *O omnia omina in anima.*

8: *Trahit sua quemque voluptas*—"Everybody's pleasure leads them their own way" (Vergil). By changing one letter (*voluptas* to *voluntas*) this was later made to mean, "Everyone's will leads them astray".

61: "Isness": being (*ens*), a scholastic concept.

110: "sea-change": *cf* Shakespeare's *The Tempest, Act I, Scene ii:*

> "Nothing of him that doth fade
> But doth suffer a sea change."

117: "Alas for the affairs of mortal men! /Such have been the doings of today", Sophocles, *Oedipus Rex.*

204: *Lucus a non lucendo*—translated in the last line of this stanza, this Latin pun means literally, "a grove because it give no light," i.e. is dark.

207: "Often afterwards but not always because"—a commensical logical proposition, (*post quod non quia propter quod*) meaning that just because one thing happens after another, it is not necessarily caused by it.

239: The last line is a translation of the last reported utterance of the Delphic Sibyl.

293: *Vale atque ave, frater*—"hail and farewell, brother!" Catullus, *Carmen ci.*

296: "Quiddity"—"whatness" or "quality", another scholastic coinage.

298: *Nox aeterna*—"eternal night".

Acknowledgements

Sections of & were first published in *Arc, Fiddlehead, Malahat Review, Poetry* (Chicago) & *Yale Review*. Thank you to the editors.

& thanks to my editor, Evan Jones, without whose painstaking & sympathetic collaboration, this poem would never have been finished.